LEGAL SYSTEMS
& INCEST TABOOS

LEGAL SYSTEMS
& INCEST TABOOS

The Transition from Childhood to Adolescence

Yehudi A. Cohen

Routledge
Taylor & Francis Group

LONDON AND NEW YORK

First published 1964 by Transaction Publishers

Published 2017 by Routledge
2 Park Square, Milton Park, Abingdon, Oxon OX14 4RN
711 Third Avenue, New York, NY 10017, USA

Routledge is an imprint of the Taylor & Francis Group, an informa business

Library of Congress Catalog Number: 2010003967

Library of Congress Cataloging-in-Publication Data

Cohen, Yehudi A.
  Legal systems and incest taboos : the transition from childhood to adolescence / Yehudi A. Cohen.
       p. cm.
  Originally published: The transition from childhood to adolescence. Chicago : Aldine, 1964.
  Includes bibliographical references and index.
  ISBN 978-0-202-36367-7 (alk. paper)
     1. Puberty rites. I. Title.

GN483.C56 2010
392.1'4--dc22

2010003967

ISBN 13: 978-0-202-36367-7 (pbk)

Speaking of transitions

this book is for

my wife

my daughter

and

my parents

CONTENTS

[7]

PART I

ONE

INTRODUCTION

T HE goal of this book is to learn why there are two distinct notions of liability in the legal systems of different societies; I propose to analyze this problem by an examination of the ways in which societies treat the transition from childhood to adolescence.

The relationships between the two sets of data — notions of legal liability, on the one hand, and the individual's evolution from childhood to adolescence, on the other — can be stated simply. The concepts of legal liability with which I shall deal — the empirical question of who assumes the onus for actions committed within a particular sociological nexus — are going to be used as independent criteria of the sense of personal responsibility. The specific ways in which different societies cope with the transition from childhood to adolescence will be examined because it is during this passage that a sense of responsibility, consonant with the goals of the society, is implanted in the growing child.

These questions and my answers lead into a second empirical problem: the universality of the incest taboos. The reason for including incest taboos in the present context can also be stated simply. The ways in which the incest taboos are taught constitute one of the crucial modes by which a sense of responsibility is implanted within an individual during his transition from childhood to adolescence.

Thus, legal systems, the transition from childhood to adolescence, and incest taboos will be my principal empirical concerns. My theoretical concerns are with the ways in which human biology and human social structures meet with, and affect, each other. Biology and social structure are both complex phenomena, and from each I shall select only a few elements on which to focus.

On the biological side, I will concentrate on a few biochemical and hormonal occurrences that seem to affect all people in all societies. Some of these events — such as the biochemical and hormonal changes that take place at the end of childhood but before adolescence begins — are well documented by medical scientists; the conjectural part of the analysis will be my theoretical extrapolations from these findings and my postulation of two stages in puberty rather than one. Moving toward the social-structural side, I shall be concerned with the psychological effects of these biochemical and hormonal changes. But these remain within the biological sphere still; the mechanisms through which psychological manifestations take place — repression, projection, displacement, isolation, denial, reaction-formation, and the like — are themselves part of the biological inheritance of the individual. Their behavioral and symbolic representations are, of course, cultural.

One of my basic assumptions is that universal physical changes in the human body at certain stages of development are accompanied by universal psychological effects. Variations arise as the result of a series of sociological and physical manipulations to which the individual is exposed during his transition from childhood to adolescence. These manipulations vary from one society to another, in each placing a unique stamp upon the psychological effects of the bio-chemical and hormonal alterations. I am attempting to say more in the latter statement than merely that each culture molds personality differently from the next: The psychological effects of the physiological changes prior to adolescence are universal predispositions, or *anlagen*; these predispositions take their final forms in adulthood as a result of highly specific manipulations of the individual by the society in which he lives. Since the number of these manipulations is extremely limited, as I shall show with respect to the ways in which a sense of responsibility is inculcated, the number of psychological outcomes is also extremely limited.

In examining incest taboos, I postulate a universal gene-carried need for "privacy". The universal incest taboos — and there are several of these, just as there are some incest taboos that are not universal — are largely designed to satisfy the need for privacy, as well as other needs. There is considerable evidence in support of the postulate of a need for privacy; this evidence also shows how a limited number of social-structural relationships, in their confluence with the need for privacy, give rise to a comparable number of universal incest taboos.

On the social-structural level, I shall be dealing with sociological boundary-maintaining systems; this general subject is my principal and continuing theoretical concern. While I am not now prepared to make any general statements on the theory of boundary-maintaining systems — much work remains before this can be done — it may be helpful to state briefly the range of the concepts involved as they are used here.

A sociological boundary-maintaining system can be described most simply by the analogy of a balloon, which is maintained by two sets of pressures in juxtaposition. If either set of pressures is changed, the balloon will collapse or expand into disintegration. Thus, the sphere maintains a boundary and becomes a boundary-maintaining system by virtue of pressures simultaneously external and internal to it. The same thing can be said of all other boundary-maintaining systems — a person, a family, a friendship, a business organization, a kin group, a community, a religion, a system of social control, and the like. Once we define the nature of the boundary and the nature of the pressures internal and external to the institution (or the person, or the community) we begin to gain insight into the dynamics of a given institution as well as various other institutions within a community.

A boundary is a limit or demarcation; events take place within it; a boundary sets off a unit (a person, a community, a group, an institution) from all other units; and individuals, influences, or objects can pass across it or be excluded by it. Boundaries vary in the extent to which they are open or closed; persons, communities, groups, and institutions may be classified into types of boundary-maintaining systems depending on the nature of the pressures that originally set them in motion and perpetuate them. But it may be stated without qualification that every thing that every person does, from birth to death, takes place within and with reference to at least one set of boundaries at any given time. This is why we speak of behavior that is "out of bounds," "beyond the pale," "off limits," and the like. It can be said that we behave differently in different institutional contexts and in different statuses (which imply different roles), but our behavior can more usefully be described as varying with different boundary-maintaining systems — that is, with different pressures surrounding or inside us.

The ways in which people mature — as, for example, the transition from childhood to adolescence — and the consequences of maturation, may therefore be seen within specific sociological boundary-maintaining systems; how incest taboos arise — and why they do not arise — may also be understood in terms of boundary systems. Nature abhors a vacuum, and the abhorrence occurs whether it is a balloon or a child on the way to becoming an adult that is being dealt with. The antithesis of a vacuum is a boundary-maintaining system, at least in human activity and in sociological structure. It is therefore a factual error to discuss any process of individual change without a careful examination of the changing individual's relationships to specific boundary-maintaining institutions and systems, whether we speak of learning role systems, of the surge of sexuality, of repression, of psychological stress and the like. When a balloon loses its boundaries, it is destroyed; when a human being loses his boundaries, he will become psychotic or die.[1*]

The specific sociological boundary-maintaining systems with which I shall deal in these cross-cultural studies are the nuclear family and the wider kin group, and the individual's relationship to them. Every society has a goal with respect to each individual's anchorage, and within which boundary-maintaining system he is to find his social-emotional identity. The kind of anchorage and identity that a person develops will determine the kind of sense of responsibility that

*Reference notes appear on pages 215-26 of this book.

[15]

will grow within him. The principal sociological nexus within which this anchorage, identity, and sense of responsibility occurs is either the nuclear family or the wider kin group. Underlying these sociological interconnections of the individual are different value systems, and evidence for the presence or absence of these value systems is to be found in each society's legal system.

Most anthropological and sociological analyses of the phenomenon of identity attempt to base their formulations on psychological theories and hypotheses. Unfortunately, however, most psychological discussions of this matter focus almost exclusively on the individual isomorphically, with little apparent awareness of the essentially social nature of identity. A crystallized identity is congruent with the goals of the society as reflected in its value system, and is rooted as much in specific boundary-maintaining systems as it is in the individual personality. Once these boundary-maintaining systems are understood, the pressures which are brought to bear on pre-pubertal individuals, for example, can be grasped more fully and their impact on personal development appreciated.

My goals here are thus twofold — empirical and theoretical. On the one hand, I shall attempt to explain some of the reasons why certain institutions exist and others do not; on the other, I shall not only attempt to illustrate the notion of boundary-maintaining systems by reference to these empirical problems, but also demonstrate that these problems could not have been solved without boundary-system theory.

As Dobzhansky has said recently,
   Man has both a nature and a 'history.' Human evolution

has two components, the biological or organic, and the cultural or superorganic. These components are neither mutually exclusive nor independent, but interrelated and interdependent. Human evolution cannot be understood as a purely biological process, nor can it be adequately described as a history of culture. It is the interaction of biology and culture. There exists a feedback between biology and cultural processes.... The fact which must be stressed, because it has frequently been missed or misrepresented, is that the biological and cultural evolutions are parts of the same natural process.[2]

Biological considerations in the study of society and culture are complex; we cannot assume an elementary one-to-one correspondence between messages transmitted through the germ plasm and cultural institutions or patterns. Biologists have been demonstrating recently, for example, that there is no simple or arbitrary relationship between one gene and one organ in the message codes which are transmitted from one generation to the next; instead, it is now generally accepted that each organ in the body contains — like a predisposition — the codes for creating all other organs, but does not carry out these messages because it lacks the necessary enzymatic structure. Thus, a human liver contains the potential to create an ear, but produces only liver tissue because it does not contain the necessary enzymatic environment to translate the "ear genes" into the organ we call an ear. It is this biological model which I shall use in the analyses of the incest taboos in Chapters 7 and 8.*

Biology is never manifest in culture in raw and pure form. Biology is always molded by culture and culture always has

*This, of course, is an oversimplified biological explanation. My purpose is simply to state a frame of reference. For a fuller elucidation by biologists see Asimov 1962, Crick 1962 and 1963, Watson 1963.

limits set for it by, among other things, human biology. To disregard biology in the study of culture is to disregard the humanness of the bearers of culture. In addition to setting limits of variation for culture to take, biology includes the predispositions that are transmitted from one generation to the next in the germ plasm; it is because some of these coded messages are universal that there are universals in culture. Without one we cannot understand the other.

The fact that wide variations do exist among societies in connection with certain types of incest taboos does not lead inevitably to the conclusion that there is no biological basis for the incest taboo. For one thing, the immediate impression of variability can be misleading; extreme differences between cultures in the same institutional realm, as between individuals, often reveal remarkable regularity and consistency when examined carefully. These regularities are to be seen in the cultural phenomena we shall consider here; and the assumption that biology and culture are inextricably bound up in their manifestations is fundamental in understanding their nature.

I am not unaware of the work of others in connection with the transition from childhood to adolescence. However, my preference is to present the results of my own research in this book and to discuss the contributions of other anthropologists elsewhere.[3]

TWO

FASHIONING AN IDENTITY
AND A SENSE OF RESPONSIBILITY

A N indissoluble relationship exists between emotional identification and a sense of responsibility. Thus, it has been observed that "the extent to which the individual feels responsible for what other people are doing, gives a clue to his degree of identification with those people."[1] Sociologically, and paralleling this psychological fact, the individual must maintain an awareness of his "self" as a discrete and unique social entity, and as separate and different in his relationships with every other person. Every culture provides the individual with a variety of means to maintain self-awareness.[2]

Every culture must make similar provision for a sense of responsibility. Consider the consequences if there were no consistent sense of responsibility in a society. How could any person maintain full self-awareness if he were unable, or were not required, to equate himself with his own actions, if he were unable to say, "I have done this," thus deriving the experience of his own being coinciding with his action? If this were to happen, social chaos would result, and personal confusion would be a consequence in the members of the group.

In order for a person to be able to care about another, he must have had the experience of having been cared for — both physically and in the sense of being important to someone else — while growing up. Similarly, in order to develop a sense of responsibility, a person must know that people have felt responsible for him, with certainty and without question. Although such early experiences are necessary for the development of the sense of responsibility, they are not sufficient.

There are many reasons why these earlier experiences of certainty are necessary to later development. For one thing, it is doubtful whether a person can develop a conscience without parents and other socializers who cared enough to set limits for his behavior and make demands on him as a child. For another, affective adult patterns are almost always built on childhood situations which serve as prototypes for later socially-expected patterns of relationship. All social relationships are reciprocal — a sense of responsibility is only one example — and adult reciprocity is, in part, built upon the emotional give-and-take of parent or surrogate, and child. Such reciprocities and feelings of certainty in children are provided for in all societies; there are many ways in which this is done, but among the most important are the physical and emotional steadiness of parents or their surrogates, and the existence of the family as a structure, with its all-important sheltering boundaries.

An example of early relationships and the child's stance with respect to the family's boundaries as prototypes of later relationships can be observed among the Navaho Indians. "The importance of his relatives to the Navaho can scarcely be exaggerated. The worst that one may say of another person is, 'He acts as if he didn't have any relatives.' Conversely, the ideal of behavior often enunciated by headmen is, 'Act as if everybody were related to you.' "[3]

Part of the preparation for such adult relationships can be observed in the early years of a Navaho's life:

> The Navaho child's emotional energy tends to be spread over a much wider surface than is the case with white children. He is not likely to have the same degree of intense emotional investment in a very few persons. Naturally, the reverse is equally true. The mother is devoted to her own children, but her feeling toward them grades off almost imperceptibly into that for her sisters' children. Her eggs are not all in one basket, emotionally speaking .... This diffuse character of Navaho social organization and of the emotional structure of Navaho society is perhaps the keynote of the whole system. Such a situation in childhood leads to and reinforces general Navaho social organization where, again, authority is highly diffuse. Just as the child's psychological security is never completely centered upon a single father or a single mother, so also no single individual is ever the sole pivot of the adult authority system. Authority is felt to be "the relatives" or "other people" or "the courts," rather than "father" or "Mr. Mustache" or "the judge."[4]

Such general principles are carried over regularly into actual behavior:

> Very striking is the extent to which even seven and eight-year-old Navahos respond passively to reprimand. The youngster who is accused of something almost never "talks back." He turns his head the other way and says nothing. Again, while one occasionally hears direct threats on the part of the parent ("I'll throw you in that water down at the dam if you aren't good"), the overwhelming tendency is to refer dis-

cipline, or the authority for it, to some individual or agency outside of the immediate family circle.[5]

A child develops his sense of self, as well as a sense of responsibility, largely as a result of the reciprocal exchanges that occur with his parents, his brothers and sisters, and his other relatives. This sense of self is one of the most crucial ingredients for his later development of a sense of responsibility, because without a clear notion of "I" a person would not be able to say, "*I* am responsible to so-and-so for this-and-that action." Reciprocally, a sense of responsibility helps to enhance the individual's awareness of self in relation to the people around him.

Among the many psychological and social attributes which children in all societies have to learn is a sense of personal responsibility congruent with the society's arrangements of values and institutions. The implantation of a sense of personal responsibility is one of the teaching-and-inculcating concerns of every society.

In bringing up their children, parents make choices from among the alternatives potentially available to them. One of the choices that is made in every society in rearing the young is between training for sociological independence or for sociological interdependence.

We usually think of independence and interdependence as characterizing individuals, either in the sense of personal attributes or in the sense of relationships between and among persons. We can also, however, think of these attributes as characterizing entire groups of people, casting the terms into a *sociological* frame. The phenomena of independence and interdependence thus viewed take place within the social fabric; they are inextricably related to other parts of the social system. Furthermore, they take place within very specific groups in the society. Thus, in the present context, "sociological interdependence" means that people within a very limited and circumscribed grouping — specifically, a kinship group — are acting upon a particular set of values with each other. (When these actions go on in a particular society, they are taking place in many such groupings simultaneously; this does not mean that all the people in a society are interdependent with each other.) Similarly, if a particular society is characterized by sociological independence, people are acting upon a quite different set of values *vis-à-vis* other members of limited and circumscribed groups in that society.

*By sociological independence, I mean that an individual's sense of responsibility is to his own nuclear family rather than to his community or to his kinsmen outside his nuclear family. By sociological interdependence, I mean that an individual's sense of responsibility lies as much with his community of kinsmen (his descent group) outside his nuclear family as it does with his nuclear family.**

A sense of responsibility is a very complex phenomenon which, upon close scrutiny, emerges as one of the central principles in social life — so much so that an individual irrevocably becomes a member of his society psychologically and culturally only when he has fully acquired the sense of responsibility which that society says he should have. A society's values are its ethic and morality. Values are postulates or premises held by the members of a society about the ways

---

*I have adopted the usages of the terms "independence" and "interdependence" from Dorothy Eggan's article (1956) on "Affect and Continuity in Hopi Cultural Conditioning," not as they were used by Birdwhistel (1958).

in which the world should be ordered — the world of man in relation to man and in relation to the material world. Values are principles of behavior which receive approbation, esteem, regard, kudos. Implicit in the ethic of any society is the tenet that action at variance with its values will incur punishment or disapprobation. "A value," in the words of the late Clyde Kluckhohn, "is a conception, explicit or implicit, distinctive of an individual or characteristic of a group, of the desirable which influences the selection from available modes, means, and ends of action."[6]

A society's value system is its declaration of how the world should be ordered and how life should be regulated. This ethic is a systematized series of statements and tenets about the ways in which people should behave toward each other, toward the unknown, toward the material world. It is a set of principles by which social arrangement and organization, order and certainty, predictability and safety are created and maintained. It is society's language, its symbolic representations of choices among alternative ways of solving the myriad problems which all people have to solve.

When values assume motive power they become such an integral part of the personality that individuals act upon them automatically, almost "without thinking". It is at this point that individuals derive deep "personal" satisfaction from being able to act on their values successfully. It is also at this point that they feel threatened and insecure when they are forced to act at variance or in contradiction to their values, or when they see others behaving according to different values.

There are certain legal onuses that are "unthinkable" to Americans and other Western peoples — such as holding a man to the possibility of capital punishment for a crime committed by his parents, wife, children or siblings. My use of the word "unthinkable" in this context is deliberate. The discoveries of psychoanalysis and other systems of psychology leave no room to doubt that what we think — what is "thinkable" and "unthinkable" — is closely tied to and mirrors emotional and personality processes of the deepest nature. What is "thinkable" and "unthinkable" in our relationships with people very clearly reflects how we feel about them and about ourselves in relationship to them.

When we say of a person that he feels responsible for another, we are implying that he is extending himself — his "self" — to that other person. To repeat, "the extent to which the individual feels responsible for what other people are doing, gives a clue to his degree of identification with those people."[7] Emotional identification is a state in which an individual takes on the characteristics and qualities of another person for himself, in which he feels one with that person, and in which he extends himself to that other person in actuality or in fantasy. In this sense, identification is a two-way process, in which the individual takes and gives emotionally. As a result, identification is a major source from which an individual derives a sense of personal identity; this is one of the ways in which an individual comes to recognize and distinguish himself and, in turn, is identified by others.

More precisely, identification is a relative concept; it involves a *degree* of feeling one with another person. Healthy and mature identification is never complete; no society could function and survive if the people in it felt completely fused with one another. Some degree of separateness and insularity is necessary in every individual if he is going to develop and mature, and some degree of separateness is necessary among individuals if separate tasks are to be allocated to them. Thus, even though people may feel responsible for each other's actions in certain societies — those whose value systems pivot around the tenet of sociological interdependence — they can never be expected to feel completely responsible for all of each other's actions.

A sense of personal identity is different from the state of emotional identification. First, a sense of personal identity is, in part, a derivative of identification as a process. Second, emotional identification is always a relationship between people, in the sense that one identifies *with* another or others. A sense of personal identity, on the other hand, is a state of being, it is a person's definition of himself ·– especially to himself — of who and what he is as a unique being; thus, a sense of identity is purely intrapsychic and refers to a person's relationship to himself. Third, although the definition and availability of the people with whom one can identify are provided by the social system, the process of identification is psychological. A sense of personal identity, however, although intrapsychic, includes sociological as well as psychological ingredients because it contains the individual's sociological placements in multiple nexuses. Thus, among the Hopi, a man's identification with his father and maternal uncle is different from his sense of personal identity as a member of a particular matrilineal clan, although the latter is in part derived from the former.

The relationship of a sense of personal identity to a state of emotional identification provides an interesting focus for studying the relationship of the individual to the society in which he lives. In this relationship, it is often difficult to separate completely psychological from sociological elements. An example can be seen in the relationship of identity to identification. While a sense of identity is purely intrapsychic, it is made up, in part, of the sociological groupings to which an individual belongs and the sociological nexuses within which he is placed. At the same time, although emotional identification occurs only between people who are available in a particular social system, or in part of it, and although identification can thus be considered a social relationship in some measure, it is still essentially a psychological phenomenon.

The establishment of a personal identity is complex and intricate. It is geared to the creation of two boundary-maintaining systems of different orders: personal and sociological.

One of the systems of needs every individual carries with him is to establish and maintain an awareness of where he begins and leaves off, and where others do so. This point has its physical components as well as its emotional and intellectual elements. Complete fusion with others means that the individual has disintegrated psychologically and is unable to function as a discrete being. A desire to maintain personal boundaries and self-awareness is biologically rooted, although the techniques vary from one culture to another. The strength of this need's pressure from within the individual can be observed in normal development, as in the child's strivings to develop a sense of "I," as well as in the most severe pathological states, such as catatonic schizophrenia, where personal boundaries and self-awareness appear to have disintegrated completely. One set of terms in which part of the process of catatonia can be understood is the ill person's feeling that he is completely isolated in a world that has disintegrated around him, and that if he "lets go" — whether of words, controls, faeces, or feelings — all will be lost to him. One of the experiences of catatonia is an absence of external pressures. The catatonic denies the existence of external or social pressures because they have become too painful for him; these pressures have ceased to exist in his reality as it is subjectively experienced, and he is fighting his collapse in a social-emotional vacuum.

The pressures for self-awareness which an individual brings to his milieu as part of his biopsychological equipment are only one aspect of the process of development of personal boundary-maintaining systems. The other part of the process is made up of the social pressures that are brought to bear on him from the social groups of which he is a member. Of course, the nature of these groups and their pressures — expectations, prescriptions, proscriptions, positive and negative sanctions, and the like — vary among societies, and even within the same society the growing individual experiences the presence and effects of different groups at various stages of development. That is, at different ages and in different groups he experiences varying pressures in the form of dissimilar routines, rewards and punishments, situations to which he is exposed and from which he is shielded, agents of socialization, and the like. These are imposed on him by his parents and by other representatives of the social system.

It is these external pressures which give final shape — consonant with the institutional and value arrangements of the society — to the individual's biopsychological strivings for identity. But these inner pressures to development are not constant or invariable. They have greater and lesser strength at different periods of childhood; the peaks rest on, or are precipitated by, a series of biologically-rooted psychological crises, and the ebbs reflect resolution of these crises. As Cumming and Cumming have put it succinctly, "the ego grows through a series of successfully resolved crises each of which disturbs a temporary equilibrium but leads to reorganization at a higher level. The ego must be thought of as in a moving steady state."[8]

There are alternative ways of looking at this over-all process of ego growth, but they are not mutually exclusive.

A number of theories of ego formation rest upon an assumption that periodic disequ'libriums between a developing child and his environment are followed by resolution and re-equilibrium at a higher level of ego organization. In this view, the normal development of a child is periodically marked by emergent biological changes that require a readaptation between him and the environment. [An] extention of this concept suggests that, at each of these periods of openness and vulnerability, a successful resolution of the crisis enhances the ego by increasing the number and variety of sets and the complexity and generality of the organization. This brings ego organization into better harmony with the increasing demands of the environment and by the same token confirms the appropriateness of this organization when it is successfully invoked in handling that environment. In contrast, failure to resolve any developmental crisis leaves a child inadequately prepared to solve future ones because he has few or poorly differentiated sets and perhaps an inadequate level of organization.[9]

This formulation describes excellently the process involved in the development of a sense of identity generally, and a sense of responsibility in particular. It will be necessary, of course, to define the nature of "the increasing demands of the environment" of which Cumming and Cumming speak, for these are not always the same; and it will also be necessary to show how the resolution of these various crises are congruent with various environmental demands.

The first source of emotional identification — and, thus, as a corallary, a sense of identity — in a person's life is in feeling one with his parents. But as a sense of separateness from parents inevitably begins to develop in him, a second major source of personal identity begins to make itself felt. This second source I shall here describe in terms of social-emotional anchorages.

Different kinds of social systems have different anchorages in sociological space for their members. Culture-and-personality studies as a rule tend to neglect this basic fact of differing institutional and value arrangements. The determination of the relationship between the socio-cultural environment and personality processes must always begin with the articulating principles of societal organization. Early socialization experiences, however important, are insufficient; certain kinds of experiences in the course of growing up, such as sleeping arrangements, dependence and independence training and the like, may suggest the types of organization that exist in the society at large, but they are not articulating social systems or sub-systems in which individuals are anchored.

Every social system works as if it assume that each of its members is going to be anchored, and thus feel anchored, at a particular point or place on the social map.[10] In some societies, it is expected in the institutional arrangements and in the value orientations that the individual will be anchored in a nuclear family — not in any specific nuclear family, but in that grouping as a boundary-system which is also a point of anchorage. In other societies, it is expected that the individual will be and feel anchored in a descent group, such as a lineage or clan. In any case, it is from his social-emotional anchorage that an individual takes his sense of identity and individuality — his awareness of who he is as a unique being and where he stands emotionally in relation to others. This anchorage is one of his major sources of "selfness." It gives him the kind of individuality that his society expects him to have, and as we shall see, there are several kinds of individuality. From the individuality that he develops, he acquires the kind of sense of personal responsibility that his society expects him to have, and there are several kinds of personal responsibility.

But social-emotional anchorage in a nuclear family is very different from anchorage in a lineage or clan. A nuclear family is a special kind of kin group: not only is it made up of both contractual and consanguineal relationships, but it is a relatively temporary arrangement. The first tie that goes to make up a nuclear family is the marital relationship, and this is a contractual bond that can be broken. The second is a blood tie, between parents and children and among siblings. While this tie can never be broken, in societies where there is no extended-family or lineage structure the nuclear family is sundered when the children marry. One of the premises on which every social system is built is that children marry and establish their own nuclear families, and this one fact places a definite limitation on people's identifications with each other in the nuclear family. There appears to inhere in the phenomenon of physical movement away from people a force that makes for social distance in the structure of relationships within the group, because it can be assumed that people will invest less emotional energy in people who may move away than in those who can be assumed to remain with the group permanently.[11]

On the other hand, a lineage — or any other descent group, for that matter — is a social unit that is devoid of contractual relationships; it is based on the only inalienable tie in life, the consanguineal. In theory, a descent group is an indissoluble unit. Therefore a descent group potentially provides a permanent anchorage for the individual and can make his sense of self coincide with the boundaries of the group.

As a result, an entirely different sense of identity — and, correlatively, a different set of institutionally relevant activities — emerges when an individual is anchored in the nuclear family, than when he is anchored in a lineage or in a clan. Briefly stated, since this will be elaborated in Chapter 6, an individual is not expected to assume responsibility for the actions of people in his nuclear family when he is anchored there, while he is expected to assume the onus for the actions of his lineage or clanmates when he is anchored in that kind of group.

A person's feelings of responsibility to others are extensions of himself — of his "self" — to others. I do not mean to imply that this "extension" is a conscious or voluntary process; it is doubtful whether people have any great degree of control over such feelings once the relevant institutional and value arrangements have been set into motion. A second implication in the term "extension" is more important: "extension" connotes "giving," and since all social relationships are reciprocal, "giving" implies "receiving." When an individual "extends" his feelings of responsibility to others he expects — and has the right to expect — other things in return. Most obviously, he expects these other persons to reciprocate his feelings of responsibility. Simply stated, this principle asserts, "If I am going to accept responsibility for your actions, I have a right to expect and to assume that you are going to feel responsible for mine."

Such a tenet of reciprocity refers, of course, to adults; rarely does it pertain to relationships between children and adults. For example, a man may be held responsible for the illegal actions of his minor son in some societies, but the minor son would be completely free of any responsibility for his father's actions. In American society, a man's responsibility for his son's actions ends when the latter becomes an adult, but at no time does the son ever assume responsibility for his father's actions. In other societies, on the other hand, a son assumes responsibility for his father's actions — as well as for the actions of others — when he himself becomes an adult. At that point, his society allows him to engage in reciprocity with his father and with other adults; as a matter of fact, his society expects and demands this of him.

The "extension" of feelings of responsibility, when it does take place, implies a particular kind of emotional relationship within a group. In a society in which an individual is not expected to extend his feelings of responsibility beyond himself we should expect to find a considerable amount of emotional insulation and isolation of the individual "self," a particular kind of emotional separateness. The emotional energies of the individual "self" in such a society tend to move in a centripetal direction and their confluence is toward the maintenance of a high valuation of the individual personality *vis-à-vis* all other personalities. Where there are such centripetal personality orientations, the society must be so constituted as to make them as effective and efficient as possible. No society can function very well if its institutional arrangements make for one type of self-system, and then turn about and expect entirely different kinds of behavior and adaptations from its members.

In a society in which an individual is expected to extend his feelings of responsibility to other persons, he not only expects reciprocal feelings of responsibility from these others toward himself, but he anticipates emotional support, acceptance, and a sense of belonging from the other members of the group and from the group as a whole. The emotional energies of the individual "self" in such a society move in a centrifugal direction and their radiation is toward the other members of the group — usually the kin group — and toward the maintenance of the boundaries of that group.

All such assertions must be taken in a relative or comparative sense. They may seem absolute in the experience of the individual members of a society, but when we view them from the outside we find such generalizations are never true in an absolute sense. For example, a Pomo Indian says, "What is a man? A man is nothing. Without his family he is of less importance than that bug crossing the trail, of less importance than the sputum or exuviae."[12] The individual is subjectively experiencing this value of his society in a total sense, but from the point of view of the observer, we know that the truth and reality of his statement are only relative. We know that he will always retain his personal identity, his own sense of "self" as a unique and discrete being; we know that he retains his personal tastes and idiosyncracies and that — short of psychosis — he will not feel that he is completely fused with another person or with the whole group. We can also anticipate that because he is human he does experience loneliness, he does at times take issue with the decisions and standards of his group, and that he does sometimes wish that he could kick over all the cultural traces that harness him in the Pomo way of life. His all-important anchorage may be in his kin group, but it is equally true and equally crucial to bear in mind that this anchorage has still another consequence: it helps to give him a sense of personal identity, a sense of "self" as separate and distinct from all other human beings.

Similarly, when an urban middle-class American speaks of the abject loneliness that arises from the conditions of his life, when he voices complaint about the isolation which the American social system forces upon him, he too is experiencing a social value in a total sense, however subjective and momentary his experience may be. Again looking in from the outside, we know that the truth and reality of his statement are only relative. We know that he has his nuclear family and sometimes his kindred; we know that he can find occupational and informal group memberships to help provide him with a sense of belonging, with a mitigation of his loneliness. He may sometimes feel that these provisions are inadequate; he may smart under the criticisms of his way of life by professional moralizers; he may at times try in many ways to kick over his traces. But he also knows that he is harnessed to a particular way of life, and that it is a way of life which does give meaning to his existence. He does have an anchorage in his family, in his occupational group, in his kindred, and so forth. It is an anchorage quite different from that a Pomo Indian; it may not be the most secure form of anchorage available to mankind, but it is an anchorage that does help create a defined social-emotional identity and sense of individuality, distinguishing the American as much as the Pomo from bugs and exuviae. And this anchorage system, with its commensurate identity and individuality, is part of his adaptation to his technology and, in turn, has consequences that can be observed in the institutional realm of his society.

How does an individual acquire his social-personal sense of anchorage, and thereby acquire the particular kind of identity and commensurate institutional behavior that he is supposed to have for effective living in his society? Words alone, however important, can never suffice in such a profound process of education. The sense of anchorage must be driven deep and implanted with such permanence and fixity that it becomes almost a "physical" part of the individual. It is one aspect of the personal counterpart of the societal value system, and its stance must be firm and irrevocable. It must become so much a part of the personality that it is not questioned; it must be open neither to debate nor to justifying rationalization. As far as the person in whom this sense is instilled is concerned, and as far as the social system cares, it *is* synthesized like an integral part of the body. As far as the cultural value system is concerned, it is a law of nature, one of the many "most obvious things in the world." The sense of anchorage must be implanted in the mind from the earliest age, constantly, at every available opportunity. And the ways in which this is done must be tied to the institutional and value structures of the society.

[36]

People learn many different kinds of things while they are children. They learn the facts of kinship that are relevant to the society in which they live, they learn how to handle their biologies and chemistries in ways that are socially acceptable, and they learn the routes, paths, byways, and symbols of their social maps. In all societies the process of moving from one person to another, from one social cell to another, from one activity to another, and the solution of different kinds of emotional, physical, social or intellectual problems require that we know how to use our sociological maps effectively. The better we know our maps, the more we understand the intricacies of the terrain, the more effectively we can move from one place to another.

Clear awareness of where one stands and from which point one is starting on any social map is indispensable for three major reasons. First is the individual's need to be economical with his energy. Second is the need of any social organization, which allocates jobs, that they be carried out as efficiently as possible. Third, predictability in social relationships provides an individual with a degree of mastery, not only in adapting to his environment but also over himself; the more certain a person is of his social relationships, the more able he is to marshal his energies and direct them into creative channels.

But no one is born knowing where he is located in social space and where he is to start on a social map. These must be learned; and this learning is so crucially important to the individual and to the social system that it must be inexorable. We turn now to how such learning occurs.

When our minds are made up about something, when we are sure of the ground on which we stand, we are less open to new ideas and knowledge than when we feel uncertain, inse-cure, vulnerable, or precarious in our stance. But children are always unsure of themselves. This is why they are so open to learning and to instruction, why teachers are so important to them and to the development of their personalities.

The establishment of social identity takes many different kinds of teaching; it is a slow, systematic, enveloping, inex-orable process of instruction, which is organized by the so-ciety to realize its own goals and to protect and incorporate the individual. This teaching takes place from the first days of life. Its impact, however, varies with the degree of the child's vulnerability and impressionability; openness to teaching is greater at some stages of development than at oth-ers. One crucial aspect of society's instruction of its young is precisely in the sociological identity of the teachers, that is, the agents of socialization. Accordingly, as I shall attempt to show, *who* a child's teachers are will help to determine where he feels anchored in social space and where he starts on his sociological map — and, thus, where his sense of per-sonal responsibility lies.

The desire of most growing boys to be like their fathers and of most growing girls to be like their mothers is one of the most important parts of the process of learning sex-iden-tity and sex-roles. There is no doubt that this desire is often fraught with considerable conflict, sometimes painful, to the children and to their parents. However important this con-flict is from certain points of view, it is largely irrelevant to understanding institutional systems and value arrangements. Furthermore, these conflicts vary considerably among soci-eties.

For example, Hsu suggests the possibility that parent-child

conflicts of this nature are stronger in American society than in traditional Chinese society. He hypothesizes that in the isolated American family, which is free of intervening structural ties, the growing child is more exposed to his parents. Hence, parents are in a position to impose their own personalities on him, and thus, to create more conflict in him. In the Chinese family, on the other hand, Hsu suggests that the family's intimate ties to the clan and to other structures protect the child from such exposure to the parents; he is thus able to grow up with somewhat greater insulation from them than the American child.[13]

But when we observe the behavior of children in relation to adults in general, including their parents, it is clear that we can broaden the notion that children wish to be like their parents: *most children want to be like—and attempt to emulate—those people who meet their needs, including those who teach them the things they want to learn.* There is evidence for this not only from the direct observation of children but from experimental biology and psychology as well; on the basis of Harlow's experiments with monkeys and other data, Scott has observed that "given any kind of emotional arousal a young animal will become attached to any individual or object with which it is in contact for a sufficiently long time."[14]*

---

*Such extrapolations from experimental work should not be taken literally; they are only suggestive for understanding human behavior. Although primates become attached to each other (and to humans), it is doubtful whether primates identify with each other emotionally as do humans. Children, like primates, become attached to others, but children have psychological needs that primates do not. In brief, the existence of patterns on lower-animal levels is never proof of their existence on the human level, unless there are also human data to make the demonstrations.

Why should this be so? Children are weak and relatively helpless; they want to grow stronger, to master skills and be able to solve tasks and problems for themselves. They often sense that if they knew more about reality, they would be less frightened. In their aspirations for strength, mastery, and skill they want to be like the adults whom they admire and whom they strive to emulate.

In discussing the economic institutions of the Southern Bantu, Richards notes that "in order to master his environment successfully, the primitive man requires institutions which shall hand on his knowledge of the technical activities required for food production, and his special experience and skill. The training of the youth of the community in these economic operations — whether by some special series of ceremonies such as initiation rites, or by more informal educative mechanisms such as example and precept — necessitates further sociological grouping. It binds the boy to those of his elders from whom he has to learn, whether these be members of his own household, or specialists from another group."[15]

This description, of course, is valid for all societies, not only primitive ones, because in the mind of a child — no matter what his societal membership — a person who teaches him knowledge that he wants to possess is a person with wisdom, and children observably idealize those who know and teach them. Such people appear to be able to do and accomplish many things — and children are still too young to be able to separate an action from the person who performs it. These are the principal mechanisms that underlie the identification of children with adults; and emulation and imitation are equally fundamental to the social-emotional anchorage that is gradually but inexorably discovered in the course of growing up.

In matrilineal societies, for example, boys not only learn from their fathers but from their mothers' brothers as well; thus, they not only wish to be like their fathers but also like their maternal uncles. Their desire to be like these uncles is further strengthened and emotionally charged by the child's realization that he belongs to the descent group of the uncles rather than to the descent group of his father. In patrilineal societies, boys learn not only from their fathers but from their fathers' brothers; and so the boys' identifications in such societies remain relatively undivided and within the lineage and the clan.

Children also learn from their parents in American society, but here there are other kinds of teachers in addition to parents and kinsmen, a situation different from that of unilineal societies. In Western countries children go to school where they learn from people who are not relatives, who are strangers to them; they leave their homes daily and learn from people with whom they have no association outside the school. What is more, they have many teachers who change year after year; thus, however much they may wish to identify with their teachers, they cannot identify with them for very long. These successive and broken identifications during the vulnerability of childhood have consequences that are consonant with the goals and values of Western society. In American society, especially, boys are taught by women and in view of the fact that children tend to identify with those who teach them, this gives rise to still other consequences.

We can observe the desire of children to learn the ways of

the adult society even among those who are designated as "learning problems." When we look closely at these children, we often find that they do in fact wish to learn — but they seek knowledge different from that which their adult mentors insist they learn. Many children with supposed "learning difficulties" are astounding in their ability to learn the batting averages of their baseball heroes, or they surpass many adults in their understanding of the mechanics of clocks and automobiles, or they know more than most laymen about space-travel. Such phenomena, of course, have very special meanings for the child psychologist or the clinician; I cite them here in order to underscore the need to learn that characterizes most children.

When a child in one society is provided with a maternal uncle with whom to identify, or with a father's brother in another society, this does not mean that the child will identify only with the figures with whom he is expected to identify. When it is said that boys learn from their fathers and their mothers' brothers in matrilineal societies, for example, this does not mean that they do not also learn from paternal kinsmen. Similarly, when we say that children in American society learn from their parents and stranger-teachers, this does not mean that they do not also learn from kinsmen as well.

In every society, predictability in adult activities as well as predictability for children is achieved, in part, by the definition and establishment of categories of individuals who are responsible for the education of the young — kinsmen who are members of the child's descent group, kinsmen who are not members of the child's descent group, non-kinsmen, and parents. From among these categories are designated the particular kinsmen for whom the socialization of youngsters is prescribed; and the child is expected to establish his basic identifications with these individuals.

For example, it is often observed in reports of patrilineal societies that a man is responsible for the education of his brothers' sons in certain areas of competence, in addition to bringing up his own children. In matrilineal societies, a man is often responsible for educating his sisters' sons, and a woman her sisters' daughters, in addition to caring for their own biological offspring.

The child will surely learn from and identify with other people as well; he will surely strive to emulate powerful figures outside the range of those "assigned" to him in his society. But in most cases, these extensions of range are in addition to the identifications necessary for the realization of the goals of the parental generation. The latter are predictable and tied to the society's institutional and value arrangements; the former are largely fortuitous and idiosyncratic.

In every social system, in other words, there are institutionally prescribed paths along which the identifications of children take place, and in each society there is a governing set of guides indicating the adults with whom a child should identify. It is through such identifications that children learn where they are anchored in social space, where their social-emotional homes are, with whom their fates are inexorably bound, and who they themselves are in their socio-cultural nexuses.

THREE

THE TWO STAGES OF PUBERTY: ESTABLISHING AN IDENTITY IN A SOCIAL NEXUS

T HERE are two stages in puberty, and each must be understood in relationship to the other — for that is how they exist and function in reality — and in relationship to the social systems in which children grow.

As children develop — physically, emotionally, and intellectually — they learn many things about the physiology and chemistry of their bodies. For a time, roughly between the ages of five to eight years, their bodily processes stabilize, and their emotions and knowledge have a chance to stabilize also. Children become stronger in all these areas, and their emotional identifications become consolidated, more certain and more consistent. But these are still the identifications of children—people who are primarily concerned with themselves, with their own feelings and needs.

It is only when children become older that they are able to relinquish some of the interests and energies focused on themselves and become aware of the needs and feelings of others. Children are capable of this achievement when they are able to give meaning to events inside their bodies and to things outside themselves, when they are able to achieve some sense of inner certainty and, therefore, of the predictability of outer things. Coinciding with this new and rather remarkable development, children are able to begin to comprehend some of the abstract concepts and principles — the values — that govern adult life; with this achievement they tend less and less to translate their needs and feelings into material actions or things. It is at this level of emotional and intellectual development that youngsters are capable of being taught, of having implanted within them the rudiments of a sense of responsibility. It is at this point that they truly start to become social and cultural beings.

During the middle of childhood, the human body begins to change rapidly again, and the child's feelings, experiences and knowledge—or, more accurately, what he once thought he knew—are no longer quite the same. The external appearances of the body remain superficially unchanged for a time but there is no longer the earlier congruence between external appearances and internal experiences and feelings.* With this discordance the first stage of puberty has dawned — but there is little on the surface of the body to identify it, little of the external appearance to explain the new dissonance of experience and sensation. The individual entering the first stage of puberty experiences confusion and great emotional and psychological vulnerability; for the society, this

---

*As I will observe in more detail later, my focus here is on the consequences of changes in the child's drive structure. There are other changes at this time, as in a growth spurt, in the replacement of milk teeth, and the like. But these are not drives and probably have different consequences from the ones being discussed here.

event provides a non-recurring opportunity to make a permanent imprint on the personality.[1]

The first stage of puberty — which begins roughly at the ages of eight to ten and which is often referred to as "latency" — consists of a series of biochemical and hormonal changes in the human body. These changes are not directly observable by the individual child or those around him, but only by biochemical assay, giving rise a few years later to the second stage in puberty, which consists of the appearance of the observable secondary sex characteristics.

I am postulating the existence of the first stage of puberty as an independent developmental episode for several reasons. First, the extraordinarily frequent occurrence of certain societal practices at about this stage of development (the subject of Chapter 4) suggests a biological regularity as a base. Second, the biochemical changes at this time are specific and circumscribed, and will be outlined. Third, as I shall attempt to show after stating some of the evidence for the existence of this discrete stage of development, these biochemical changes appear to produce their own psychological consequences and transcend particular cultures.

The specific changes within the child that constitute the first stage of puberty begin with the production of androgens and gynogens. Medical research workers such as Kunstadter,[2] Kenyon, Knowles and Sandeford,[3] and Whitelaw and Foster,[4] — working with human subjects — have been able to demonstrate consistently that the later appearance of secondary sex characteristics can be controlled by the administration of specific adrogens and gynogens between the ages of eight to ten or eleven years. These hormonal administrations not only produce changes through the broad spectrum of genital development but also, as shown by Whitelaw and Foster, they produce such extragenital anabolic effects as increases in height and bone age.*

Parallel to these findings is the work of experimental psychologists and biologists dealing with critical periods in behavioral development.[5] The work of investigators in this area of research must be approached cautiously for an understanding of the transition from childhood to adolescense, at least for the present, because most of these studies deal only with infancy and early childhood, as well as relying heavily on research with animals. However, the tentative conclusions of students of critical periods of development are very suggestive for an appreciation of some of the processes involved in later childhood and in the transition to adolescence.

In reviewing and summarizing the salient investigations in this field of study, Scott has observed:

The basic timing mechanisms for developmental periods are obviously the biological processes of growth and differentiation, usually called maturation. . . .

[One] approach to the problem is to try to identify the actual mechanisms which open and close a period. Since an important part of forming a primary social relationship appears to be emotional arousal while the young animal is in contact with another, it is obvious that the critical period for socialization could be timed by the appearance of behavioral mechanisms which maintain or prevent contact, and this is indeed the case. . . .

Thus, understanding the process of socialization and its

---

*Bone age refers to a method for examining the wrist-bones of prepubescent children by X-ray and, from this, determining the potential for height that the child can achieve.

timing mechanisms in any particular species requires a systematic study of the development of the various capacities which affect the time of onset and the duration of the critical period....

In short, it seems likely that the formation of a social attachment through contact and emotional arousal is a process that may take place throughout life, and that *although it may take place more slowly outside of certain critical periods,* the capacity for such an attachment is never completely lost....

At this point, we can only state a provisional general hypothesis: that *the critical period for any specific sort of learning is that time when maximum capacities — sensory, motor, and motivational, as well as psychological ones — are first present....*

Both growth and behavioral differentiation are based on organizing processes. This suggests a general principle of organization: that once a system becomes organized, whether it is the cells of the embryo that are multiplying and differentiating or the behavior patterns of a young animal that are becoming organized through learning, it becomes progressively more difficult to reorganize the system. That is, organization inhibits reorganization. Further, organization can be strongly modified only when active processes of organization are going on, and this accounts for critical periods of development....

Some data suggest that for each behavioral and physiological phenomenon there is a different critical period in development.... There is evidence that critical-period effects are more common early in life than they are later on, and that the critical period for primary socialization is also critical for other effects, such as the attachment to particular places, and may overlap with a critical period for the formation of basic food habits."[6]

In speaking about the changes in the body during the first stage of puberty, I confine myself to biological drives that emerge epigenetically. There is, of course, a growth spurt during middle childhood in which, for example, milk teeth are lost and are replaced by adult teeth; some societies attach great importance to such events. But societies can attach great importance to almost anything; the idiosyncrasies of individual cultures, important in themselves for a variety of other purposes, are not the focus of my present concern. My interest here is with the interaction between the growing individual and members of his society when the drive structure and organization of his body changes to precipitate a congenital critical period of development, and with the consequences, for the individual as well as the society, of bodily changes that occur in all people by reason of their physiological constitution. Such phenomena as growth spurts and the emergence of adult tooth-structure are not biological drives, and their relationships to institutions, values, and customs require altogether separate analyses.

The first stage of puberty, with its revolutionizing biochemical and hormonal changes is very confusing for the child because, while he senses that something is going on inside him, he cannot see what is happening. The second stage of puberty, which consists of the emergence of the observable secondary sex characteristics, produces somewhat less confusion in pubescent individuals because they can see change in their bodies. Therefore, it can be anticipated that the relatively lesser degree of confusion during the second stage of puberty decreases the opportunity for societies to implant values and attitudes.

If this latter postulate is valid, then — and this is my first hypothesis — it should also follow logically that *more societies will take formal and explicit steps in connection with the first stage of puberty than with the second stage, and that whatever steps are taken in connection with the first stage will be more drastic than those taken in connection with the second stage.* In more concrete terms, adolescent initiation ceremonies, for example, which usually take place during the second stage of puberty, will be less drastic in their effects than the comparable steps taken in connection with the first stage. Fewer societies will subject their youths to initiation ceremonies during the second stage than will subject their children to comparable experiences during the first stage of puberty.

These "comparable experiences" are described in Chapters 4 and 5 below. Meanwhile, I offer a derivative, second hypothesis: *The climax of fixing an individual's anchorage and establishing his sense of social and emotional identity and selfhood will occur at the first major point of confusion after early childhood — that is, at the first stage of puberty — and it will take place through manipulations of the child's relationships with his nuclear family.*

The social system uses these relationships because the nuclear family forms the center and provides the boundaries of the world of the child. But every child must also have his horizons broadened; he must be taught that his nuclear family is not the entire world, and that there are other people and other institutions with whom he must cooperate and in which he must participate.

The nuclear family is everywhere a kin group that is part of a larger kinship system. But there are also many instances in which the nuclear family merges into a larger kinship system, as in extended-family organization. And in many of the latter instances, the education of children in defined areas of knowledge or competence by designated extra-familial kinsmen is prescribed.

Since children identify with those people who teach them, we should expect to find that where children are taught both by their parents and by kinsmen outside the nuclear family, these children will identify both with their parents and with their kinsmen who are also their teachers. But we should also expect that since parents are more important to children than are kinsmen outside the nuclear family, and since parents generally teach more than anyone else, the strongest identifications of a growing child will be with his parents. Therefore, if a society wants its growing members to acquire an anchorage outside the nuclear family, it is going to have to do something to interfere with or weaken a child's identification with his parents.

Furthermore, if it is true that feelings of identification in a society are expressed in institutionally relevant and meaningful activity, then — and this is my third hypothesis — *the kinds of manipulations of the child's relationships to his nuclear family at the first stage of puberty will be closely tied to the persons who bring him up and teach him and to the kinds of values that must be inculcated in him for the preservation of the society's goals.*

Thus, what happens to a child at the first stage of puberty

in terms of his relationships to his nuclear family is directly related to the persons who teach him or are involved in his upbringing prior to the first stage of puberty — that is, for the first eight, nine, or ten years of his life. And the persons who teach a child for these years are directly related to the kinds of values which the society says the child should have.

The three hypotheses thus far put forward deal with the psychological and sociological phenomena of the first stage of puberty. But there is still the biochemical aspect of puberty, the root of it all. Though there are many aspects of biochemical changes during the first stage, I will only be concerned here with the sexual.

The biochemical changes of the first stage of puberty rapidly cast sexuality into a sociological lineament in addition to a personal one, because coitus and reproduction soon become possible. In prospect of this, parents must now begin to cope with their children's sexuality — and nascent heterosexuality — in sociological terms. And as far as any social system is concerned, the first rule of sexual life is the incest taboo.

In most of the world's societies, children have recurrent opportunity to observe their parents in sexual intercourse. This is so because of the ways in which houses are built and because of customary sleeping arrangements. Very few societies seem to insist that parents and children be separated at night by walls and doors. But even when a society does manifest the custom of separating parents and children, it not infrequently happens that children are put to sleep in the parents' rooms and thus retain opportunity to observe them in sexual intercourse.

It is safe to assume that such observation is sexually

arousing and exciting for most children. Because parents have to begin coping with the sexuality of their children in the first stage of puberty, they must for the first time consider the possible effects on the children of such observation. Children can be sexually attracted to their parents prior to the first stage of puberty, but after this stage they are capable of acting on their attractions. In addition, sexual attraction to siblings can now be acted on, and siblings, like parents, are always sexually taboo.

Observation of parental intercourse is not the only source of sexual arousal in children. The internal biochemical secretions give rise to sexual excitation autonomously. These autonomous sources of sexual arousal produce the possibility — a danger, as far as society is concerned — that sexual feelings will be directed overtly to parents and siblings.

As a result of the convergence of social interdicts and the impending ability to act on sexual feelings — *the climax of inculcating the incest taboo in the child must take place early in the first stage of puberty.* Children certainly have fantasies of marrying their parents or siblings prior to the first stage of puberty. However, it is doubtful whether most children are aware of the sexual connotations of marriage. Furthermore, since most young children almost invariably place this fantasy in the future, the first stage of puberty appears to be the most likely time to encourage the relinquishment or the repression of the fantasy.

The simplest way to cope with children who are directing their sexual excitation to members of the nuclear family is to remove them physically from the family. This is precisely what is done in many of the world's societies, as we shall see in the next chapter.

FOUR

CEREMONIES OF THE FIRST
STAGE OF PUBERTY:
EXTRUSION AND
BROTHER-SISTER AVOIDANCE

Aɴ examination of the sample of societies used in this investigation — the data for which are presented at the end of this and in the following two chapters — reveals that one of two courses regarding the manipulation of children is followed at the first stage of puberty. One choice is to interfere with or impose a discontinuity upon the child's relationships to his family of orientation. Alternatively, these ties may be allowed to remain undisturbed, in which case other measures have to be taken in order to establish an anchorage within the family's boundaries.

The disruption of a child's relationships to his family may occur in one of two ways or both; they are not mutually exclusive. The child may be subjected to either of the institutionalized customs of *extrusion,* or *brother-sister* avoidance.

"Extrusion" refers to the physical dislodgment of the child from the household early in the first stage of puberty, that is, between the ages of eight to ten years. In societies in which extrusion occurs, the child usually spends the entire day with his family but goes to sleep elsewhere at night; the basic rule underlying the custom is that the child cannot sleep under the same roof as his parents. In a few societies, such as the Andamanese and the Tikopia, the child is informally adopted at the first stage of puberty by friends or distant kinsmen of his parents and goes to live in their households, returning to the parental home for periodic visits. Where children are not adopted by friends or distant relatives, they sleep at night in a hut which has been built for this purpose, in a men's house or bachelor's dormitory, on the roof of the house, in the open around a fire which burns all night for warmth and protection from wild animals, and so forth.* In any case, the extrusion of the child from the household is usually carried out within the existing structure of the household or community. The illustration on page 56, reproduced from Meyer Fortes' *The Web of Kinship Among the Tallensi,* is one example (from West Africa) of the way in which this is often done; note the location of the "Do'o," the room for adolescent boys.[1]

---

*Among the Nyakyusa, as among the Lamba (see below), extrusion is carried to an extreme in the establishment of "age villages" (Wilson 1951). The Nyakyusa are not part of the sample of societies in the present study (see chapter 9), but the data for them are in accord with the hypotheses of this inquiry. Furthermore, turning parenthetically to still another society, the custom among the English upper class of sending children to boarding schools is not a form of extrusion. Usually, under the latter circumstances, children are permitted to sleep under the same roof as their parents when they are home during vacations and holidays. The English upper-class custom of taking or sending children abroad during holidays and vacations might be a survival from ancient English clans, in which extrusion was practiced, but there is no rule in England today that children may not sleep under the same roof as their parents. If this were truly extrusion, they would not be permitted to do so.

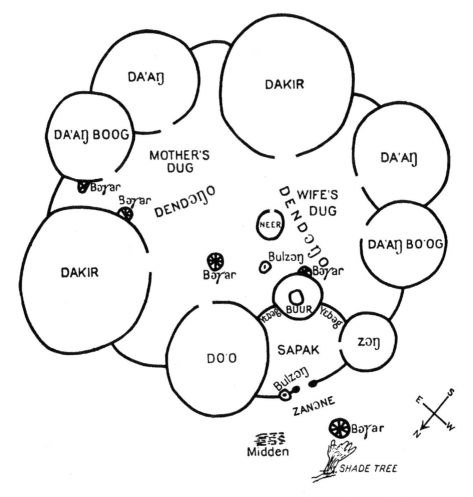

FIG. 2b. Diagram of Ɔndieso's homestead, showing the layout of the quarters and the rooms. (Scale: 1:45 approx.)

Glossary

Bɔɣar	Ancestor shrine
Buur	Granary
Bulzɔŋ	Shelter for hens
Da'aŋ	Unroofed dry-season kitchen
Da'aŋboog	Storeroom and wet-season kitchen
Dakir	Sleeping-room
Do'o	Room for adolescent boys
Dɛndɔŋo	Open courtyard
Sapak	Livestock yard
Zanɔne	Open space at the gateway where the men foregather
Zɔŋ	The homestead head's special room
Neer	Grinding-room
Yɛbɔg	Low dividing wall

In most of the societies in which it is practiced, extrusion ends with the marriage of the child. This is extremely significent from two points of view. First, it points clearly to the sexual factor that seems to underlie the custom. Second, if the rule of extrusion were not rescinded at the time of marriage, many societies would be unable to maintain extended families, as the child would be forced to continue to sleep away from his parents' household.

Most societies that practice extrusion dislodge the boys. In a few societies, both the boys and girls are extruded. In a very small number of societies, only the girls are extruded from the parental household.

"Brother-sister avoidance" refers to a prohibition of contact or interaction between brother and sister.* Where brother-sister avoidance is practiced, the rule usually states that brother and sister are not allowed to speak to each other directly after the older of them has reached the first stage of puberty; if they must communicate with each other, the rule usually states that they may only do so through a third party. They may not touch each other, they may not look at each other, and they may not be alone under the same roof at any time of day or night even if they are not looking at each other. Very often, the rule of brother-sister avoidance goes on to state that if the two are walking along a road and should happen to meet, one must turn away until the other has passed.

Brother-sister avoidance usually but not always ends upon the marriage of one or both of the siblings; there are, how-

---

*A separate cross-cultural study, on which I shall not report here, shows that there is no relationship between brother-sister avoidance and parent-in-law avoidance. The two avoidance patterns are entirely different.

ever, instances in which the rule continues beyond the marriage of both. I have not been able to find any reasons for the continuation of the rule beyond marriage. Extrusion and brother-sister avoidance sometimes occur in the same society. Here, too, I have not been able to uncover any conditions under which the two necessarily go together or any conditions which would require that one be present without the other.

Cumming and Cumming, addressing themselves to clinical goals, observe that "ego growth is essentially a series of disequilibriums and subsequent re-equilibrations between the person and the environment. Therefore, by extension, it seems reasonable that growth might be induced by presenting the individual with a series of graded crises under circumstances that maximize his chance of resolving them."[1a] Although this formulation was originally intended for the manipulation of the environment of a mental hospital to facilitate ego re-equilibrium in patients, it is also a highly suggestive insight for understanding socio-cultural processes. The clinical situation is a slice of life in intensity or in variety, and what follows in one should follow in the other.

Extrusion and brother-sister avoidance confront children with a crisis in their orientations to the world and in their relationships to their families — that is, in their ego development. However, there seem to be certain processes or states of mind in children of this age that make them somewhat amenable or psychologically open to such arrangements.

For example, it is at roughly this age that boys and girls usually begin to segregate themselves from each other and at which they tend to become shy in each other's presence, even where segregation does not occur. And it is roughly at this stage of development that children begin to experiment with different kinds of personal identities.

When children begin this experimentation — a process that accelerates remarkably during and after the second stage of puberty — they are striving for many goals. For example, when Crow Indian boys play at archery, at hunting rabbits and birds, at warfare and scalping large animals that serve as "enemies," or when they establish clubs patterned on the men's organizations, they are gaining insight — compatible with their maturational levels — into life as an adult male Crow. Young girls among the Crow begin to practice at life as Crow women when they play with little shields, just as their mothers are the custodians of the real ones; similarly, a six- or seven-year old girl plays at sexual roles, in which she visits a boy and, after his family gives her something to eat, lies down with him as though she were his wife.

Similarly, when a Western child says one day that he is going to be a taxi driver and the next day that he is going to be an astronomer, he is wondering, "What would it be like or feel like to be this or that?" And when he rejects one kind of occupation or vocation for another he is thereby learning a little bit at a time who he is and what he is, what kind of person he is becoming and what kind of person he would like to be.*

Through such fantasy activity, the child as a social person

---

*An important consideration, in the comparative study of ego development, is that the Western child has many more fantasies *available* to him than the non-Western child. In non-industrialized societies, there are extremely few mantles of identity from which to choose.

is trying to find a place for himself in social "space." He is at the first stage of locating himself outside the world of parents and siblings, outside the boundaries of the nuclear family. The form of his personality, separate and appropriately insulated and contained, is beginning to acquire the contours that will distinguish him from all other persons. But all of this, of course, must take place in a way that is appropriate to the social system in which he is going to live as an adult.

In the development of a sense of personal identity there are two wellsprings from which an individual draws: the personal and the social. Both of them converge in each human life; they flow into each other constantly in every individual's growth and maturation. They are so inextricably bound that it is sometimes difficult to tell them apart. Neither can exist without the other, and both are so necessary to the individual that they are also indispensable to each other. Unless the society's institutional organization can work with the child's needs to mature, it can not make its indelible impressions on the growing person. Similarly, the child's need to find a personal identity or sense of self would be aimless without the orienting targets of social goals, without the reality of a sense of social belonging, and without the meaningfulness of a particular kind of life with other people.

The particular ways in which a child's relationship to his family — and to the kinship space around the family — are manipulated in the society provide the tools with which his strivings for a sense of identity and autonomy are shaped. These ways, however, are also limits set for the child within the social system in which he is growing up. They say to him, in effect, "These are the directions in which you may move to establish your identity, this is the part of the social terrain in which you may stake out a claim as a social, cultural, and psychologically unique being." Just as these limits direct the growing person to a realization of his needs for autonomy and selfhood, as boundaries they restrict him from finding an anchorage that is incompatible with the society's goals.

As we have observed, children tend to identify emotionally with those who instruct them in the ways of their society. Thus, who teaches the young is even more important in this context than what is taught them. Take, for example, one of the most important facts of the universe about which children learn: the kinship system of the society in which they are growing up and in which they are going to live as adults. They learn the terminology of kinship and the behavior that reflects the ethical mannerisms of the kinship system; they also learn that their nuclear families occupy definite positions — physical and social — within a total social and kinship space. But beyond learning explicit and formal kinship data, a child learns about kinship in implicit ways. If he is consistently taught by his mother's brother and is told that he must heed and obey that man *because* he is his mother's brother, this sets a clear stage for the child's identification with his maternal uncle. There are surely idiosyncratic factors that can make the identification strong or weak in any individual case, but it can be assumed that, in any event, some degree of identification with the mother's brother will be set into motion.

If the child's mother's brother is also a disciplining agent, whatever energies the child has for identification will be distributed among his parents, who teach him the most, and his mother's brother. And when the child observes and is taught that he is a member of a kin group (a boundary-maintaining system) to which he, his mother and her brother belong — but to which his father does not belong — this will give even more impetus to his identification with his maternal uncle.

By observing, and by being taught that his identity is found along the matrilineal line and that his anchorage is in a matrilineal kin group and not in the nuclear family alone, the child begins to acquire an awareness of the persons with whom his emotional lot lies. But however important such experiences are, they are not enough; a sense of anchorage can only be acquired by the manipulation and distribution of his energies for identification in relation to the boundaries of particular kin groups.

This must be done for two reasons. First: When a society manipulates a child's emotional identifications so that he can develop an anchorage in a kin group, it does not intrude into the child's identifications with individuals; instead, it maneuvers the child in relation to the boundaries of specific kin groups. Groups are, of course, made up of people, but as soon as aggregates of individuals acquire boundaries, they become more than the sum total of the persons in the group. Thus, as we shall see, when a society which brings up its children for sociological interdependence interferes with a child's identification with his nuclear family so that he can develop an anchorage within the kin group, it is not weakening or even attempting to weaken the child's identification with his parents; nor, on the other hand, is it attempting to strengthen the child's emotional identifications with any particular kinsmen outside his family. What it is attempting is to deflect the child's energies from within the boundaries of the family into the boundaries of the kin group.

Second: Human families contain the potentiality of "emotional inbreeding,"[2] a tendency in some groups — usually small ones — for their members to concentrate all their emotional energies on each other and within the group boundaries to the relative exclusion of outsiders. This is a tendency — which can be found in almost any kind of group — to glorify one's own group above all others, to see it as the only possible source of emotional and social satisfaction, and to see other groups as unsatisfying or even threatening. A society whose value system requires that individuals find their anchorage in the wider kin group cannot allow individual nuclear families to become emotionally inbred.[3]

Such inbreeding is usually seen in most intense form in the nuclear family; the first and most compelling identifications and attachments of the child are defined in terms of the family's members and its boundaries, to the relative psychological exclusion of outsiders. To extend the child's awareness of his identity to a larger kin group requires more than observation and teaching alone; the achievement of this displacement must be accomplished by physically forceful and visible events. Herein lies the sociological significance of the phenomena of extrusion and brother-sister avoidance.

For both these reasons, if the potentiality for emotional inbreeding within the family is to be minimized, steps must be taken at a time when the individual is psychologically open to such influence — when he is most ready to acquire a culturally appropriate sense of identity and a concomitant social-emotional anchorage. Similarly, if, in the value system of a society, an individual's anchorage and identification must remain within the nuclear family, the potentiality for emotional inbreeding must be left relatively undisturbed, at least as far as the individual's sense of identity and anchorage is concerned. And here, too, a physical action will be taken at the first stage of puberty, by leaving the child within the boundaries of the nuclear family.

In discussing some of these issues from the point of view of the mutuality of conflict and cohesion in the structure of society, Gluckman observes that in some societies, "while on the one hand the members of the family are brought together by [customary] rules, on the other they are forced apart and estranged from one another."[4] He suggests that "these estrangements within the African family are related to the cohesion of the larger society."[5] In discussing taboos, he says they "are also important because they introduce divisions — estrangements — into the family and prevent it absorbing the wholehearted emotional allegiance of its members. Husbands are forced apart from their wives to continued association with their own kin, and children turn toward more distant kin and away from their parents. The estrangements in the family are associated with the extension of ties to wider kinship groupings."[6] Applying this hypothesis to data of the Nuer, Gluckman concludes, and the present study bears him out cross-culturally, that "this implies that the family itself demands allegiance *at the expense* of the wider kinship group — and obviously also that the wider kinship groups demands allegiance at the expense of the family."[7]

The patterns of identification that have been instilled in

a child for the first seven or eight years of his life — regardless of the society in which he is being reared — are relatively weak; they have not developed out of any crisis within the child or out of any exigency in relation to the family in which he lives. To graft an enduring pattern of identification and a sense of anchorage onto his personality, there must be an accessibility to his thinking, his ways of feeling, his relationship to himself and to others. This vulnerability in the individual accompanies the biochemical changes and their attendant confusion at the first stage of puberty.

And since these disquieting physiological and psychological changes are unlike anything that has happened before, new measures — unlike any in the past — must be taken in order to give the child's sense of identity a climactic casting and a lasting adhesiveness to a particular set of sociological boundaries. But however different these new steps are, they must be in harmony with the values and social prescriptions previously instilled.

If parents in a society try to bring up their children so that they will be anchored in the larger kin group instead of only within the family, they must see to it that the rearing is shared by members of the children's descent group, so that the children can establish emotional identifications with the wider grouping of kinsmen. But since every human family contains within it the potentiality of emotional inbreeding, this sense of anchorage in the larger kin group must receive its climactic impetus from a physical manipulation of the child in relation to his family. This leads directly to my fourth hypothesis, which is in two parts:

(1) *In those societies in which children are being brought up for sociological interdependence, that is, anchorage and*

identification in the wider kin group, they will be brought up and taught by members of the child's descent group as well as by the parents; and during the first stage of puberty there will be a physical disruption or discontinuity in the child's relationships to his family — through extrusion or brother-sister avoidance or both.

On the other hand, if the parents in a society try to bring up their children to be anchored within the family so that their primary identifications will remain within the boundaries of that group, these parents will have to insure that their children's upbringing remains principally in their own hands. Since children must be taught by other people in addition to their parents, the other teachers in societies in which children are brought up for sociological independence cannot come from any boundary-maintaining group — such as a lineage or a clan — with which there may develop a strong and lasting emotional identification. Therefore, in such a society, children can be brought up by their parents as well as by kinsmen who are *not* members of the child's descent group, or by their parents as well as non-kinsmen or strangers, such as schoolteachers. And, again, we would expect that in such a society a child's relationship with his nuclear family during the first stage of puberty would not be disturbed. The child's sense of anchorage or identification with the family, intensified by the inevitable tendency toward emotional inbreeding, would receive its climactic impetus by allowing the child to remain within the family without interruption and without discontinuity. Thus, the second half of my fourth hypothesis:

(2) *In those societies in which children are being brought up for sociological independence, that is, anchorage and*

identification in the nuclear family, they will be brought up by non-members of the child's descent group as well as by their parents; and during the first stage of puberty there will be physical continuity without interruption in the child's relationship to his family.

In a patrilineal society in which children are being brought up for sociological interdependence, that is, anchorage and identification in the wider kin group, the children's upbringing is assigned to patrilineal kinsmen, in addition to their parents, in specified areas of competence, such as technological, ritual, mythological or other kinds of knowledge. Maternal kinsmen might also be assigned tasks of socialization in such a patrilineal society, but it is the prescriptions surrounding the patrilineal kinsmen — as effective representatives of the society's articulating principles of organization — that concern us here. (The reverse can also be true in a matrilineal society.) Prescribed instruction by maternal kin in a patrilineal society organized around the values of sociological interdependence — or by paternal kin in a matrilineal society — does not interfere with the identifications and anchorage in the patrilineal group, because the latter is a boundary-maintaining system, whereas the maternal kin in a patrilineal society do not constitute such a system. (I will return to this problem in Chapter 8.)

To repeat a principle stated earlier: no attempt is made to weaken or interfere with the child's identification with his parents when he is directed toward developing an anchorage within the kin group. The attempt, rather, is toward a deflection of the child's energies for identification from within one set of sociological boundaries (the family) into another (the kin group). A sense of anchorage is very different — and at a somewhat different level of abstraction — from dyadic identifications, because the sense of anchorage develops within a boundary-maintaining system that exists before the individual is born and continues as part of the social system long after he departs. At best, a dyadic identification establishes a unique and temporary boundary-system which is coterminous with the two individuals alone. This is one reason for attaching particular importance to the concept of boundary-maintaining systems in understanding these socio-cultural phenomena.

There are twenty-eight societal or community units, in the sample of sixty-five used for this study, in which children are brought up by their parents plus members of the child's descent group.[8] In many of these societies children are also reared by kinsmen who are not members of their descent group, but, as stated earlier, I am primarily concerned with the core of parents-plus-members-of-the-child's-descent-group. In all these societies, children are subjected to the experiences of either extrusion or brother-sister avoidance, and three societies display both extrusion and avoidance. The ethnographic data are presented after the statistical materials below.

Twenty-two of these societies are sedentary and six are nomadic; eighteen are characterized by patrilineal descent, seven by matrilineal descent, and three by bilateral descent.

Of the thirty-seven societies in which children are brought up by their parents plus non-members of their descent groups, only one (the aboriginal Omaha) has the custom of extrusion at the first stage of puberty.

Tables 1 through 4 summarize these data and present the statistical verification of the hypotheses presented thus far.

Table 1*

Relationships between Agents of Socialization and Experiences at the First Stage of Puberty

	Extrusion and/or br-si avoidance	No extrusion or br-si avoidance
Socialization by parents plus members of child's descent group	28	0
Socialization by parents plus non-members of child's descent group	1	36
$x^2 = 57.19$	$T = .94†$	$p < .001$

*Because of the small frequencies in at least one of the cells in each of the tables, the Yates correction has been used in the following Chi-square calculations.

†For Kruskal's T, see W. J. Dixon and F. J. Massey, Jr., Introduction to statistical analysis. New York, McGraw-Hill, 1951.

Table 2

Relationships between Agents of Socialization and Extrusion at the First Stage of Puberty

	Extrusion	No extrusion
Socialization by parents plus members of child's descent group	26	2
Socialization by parents plus non-members of child's descent group	1	36
$x^2 = 49.69$	$T = .82$	$p < .001$

Table 3

Relationships between the Structure of Descent
Groups and Agents of Socialization

	Unilinear descent groups	No Unilinear descent groups
Socialization by parents plus members of child's descent group	25	3
Socialization by parents plus non-members of child's descent group	19	18
$x^2 = 9.62$	$T = .34$	$p < .02$

Table 4

Relationships between the Structure of Descent Groups
and Experiences at the First Stage of Puberty

	Extrusion and/or br-si avoidance	No extrusion or br-si avoidance
Unilinear descent groups	26	18
No unilinear descent groups	3	18
$x^2 = 9.90$	$T = .39$	$p < .02$

[70]

An examination of the statistical values in these four tables reveals progressively decreasing values. Thus, there is statistical support for the hypothesis that experiences of the first stage of puberty, in general, are strongly tied to the identity of the agents of socialization. Slightly less significant, though of great importance, is the relationship between the agents of socialization and the presence or absence of unilineal descent groups; and, as would be expected from this, the relationship beween experiences at the first stage of puberty, in general, and the presence or absence of unilineal descent structure as an articulating principle of the social system is of almost equal significance.

The following are the societies of the sample in which children are brought up for sociological interdependence:

The *Andaman Islanders* are a Negrito people living in the eastern part of the Bay of Bengal, now within the state of India. The Andamanese are nomadic hunters and gatherers and practice no agriculture; fishing provides an important staple in their diet. There are no lineages or clans among the Andamanese; the band is composed of nuclear families, most of which share kinship connections in common, especially as a result of the tendency of brothers to build their huts next to each other. Descent among the Andamanese is bilateral and residence upon marriage is neolocal. For the greater part of childhood, children are brought up by their parents plus maternal and paternal kinsmen in the band who have definite educative functions with respect to these youngsters.[9]

"At the age of ten, or a little before, a change is often brought about in the life of a child, owing to the custom of adoption."[10] This custom stipulates that at about the age of

[71]

ten, a boy or a girl is adopted by a man and his wife living in a different band. "The adopted child lives with his or her foster-parents, having a place in their hut and a share of their meals. From about the age of ten children of both sexes begin to be of service to their parents or foster-parents in many ways. The foster-parents treat their adopted children in exactly the same way that they would treat their own children, and the children on the other hand show the same regard and affection to their foster-parents that they do to their own parents, and assist them in every way that they can. Their own parents come to visit them at regular intervals."[11]

The *Chiricahua Apache* of southeastern Arizona were organized into hunting bands. Kinship was reckoned bilaterally, but there was a slight tendency toward a matrilineal emphasis. Residence upon marriage was matrilocal, and most families within the band were related to each other. A child's maternal grandparents were intimately involved in his socialization, and a child's mother's brother was especially involved in his education;[12] paternal kinsmen had the job of teaching a boy the ways of hunting and warfare.

The Apache did not practice brother-sister avoidance; and although there was no formal rule concerning extrusion, families usually built a separate dwelling for a boy where he "can stay if he should find his sister the sole occupant of the family dwelling."[13]

The *Arapesh*, a Papuan people of Northeast New Guinea, are sedentary agriculturalists who live in patrilineal clan-communities. The education of children is principally in the hands of parents, but paternal kinsmen also share significantly in a child's upbringing.[14] There is no extrusion for boys, but there is extrusion for girls. When an Arapesh girl is betrothed at about the age of seven or eight years, she goes to live in her future husband's village and becomes part of his parent's household; usually, this is about a day's walk from her parental village. She returns to the latter community only occasionally.

The *Arunta* of Australia are nomadic hunters and gatherers who live in loosely organized bands, each of which has its own territory. The band is usually made up of two or three nuclear families, the heads of which are brothers. Reckoning their descent patrilineally, these brothers are intimately involved in the rearing and education of each other's children.[15]

The Arunta practice a limited form of brother-sister avoidance. "A man may speak freely to his elder sisters in blood, but those who are tribal [classificatory] sisters must only be spoken to at a considerable distance. To younger sisters, blood and tribal, he may not speak, or at least, only at such a distance that the features are indistinguishable."[16] Also, a few years before the appearance of secondary sex characteristics a boy goes through the first of a series of *rites de passage*; this ceremony is called "Throwing the Boy Up in the Air." When a few boys have been assembled who are at the proper age for this ceremony, they are thrown individually into the air several times by the older men of the band; the women of the group are permitted to attend.

The *Bantu* of North Kavirondo (principally the *Logoli* and *Vugusu*) live in the westernmost portion of Kenya. Their social groupings are the patrilocal extended family, the patrilineal lineage, and the patrilineal clan-community. Most households are polygynous and a child comes under the influence of his mother; at the same time, however, the father plays a large role in bringing up his children, as do the father's brothers and other patrilineal kin. The mother's brother does play a role in a child's upbringing, but his part is minor.[17]

"Children of both sexes sleep in the house of their parents until they are about six years old. At that age their lower incisors are knocked out and they are thereby initiated into the second phase of childhood. They sleep now in the house of a widowed grandparent, and a year or two later a son moves into the . . . bachelor hut of an elder brother or friend, while a daughter sleeps in the . . . unmarried girls' hut."[18] The unmarried girls' hut is usually supervised by a real or fictive grandmother who controls the girls' moral conduct. During the day, boys and girls are under the control of their parents and eat with their parents.

The *Basuto* of the Union of South Africa are an agricultural people who also practice a considerable amount of husbandry; they reside in permanent villages. The social groupings of the Basuto are the nation (ruled over by a Paramount Chief), the patrilineal clan, the village, and the patrilocal extended family. The clan is neither a localized nor a corporate group. Authority over children was exercised principally by the father, but children also came under the consistent educative influences of patrilineal kinsmen outside the family; "one is usually brought up amongst these people,"[19] and paternal kinsmen of different categories have particular duties in contributing to a child's upbringing.[20] Under the impact of European influences, clan organization has weakened considerably as has the educative function of the clan for the child; these influences have also weakened the father's authority over his children.[21]

Traditionally, young boys had to sleep in the bachelors' hut, the youngest of whom "might occasionally sneak home to be cossetted and petted by their mothers and given tit-bits of food. Today much of this discipline has been re-laxed"[22] and youths often stay at home. Extrusion was not practiced for girls.

The *Bena* are a patrilineal people living north of Lake Nyasa in Tanganyika. The rearing of children is shared among parents, paternal and maternal kinsmen. "Here, how-ever, a reservation must be made regarding those cases where the maternal and paternal relatives are of dissimilar social position; for when one side of the family is, say, of royal blood and the other of common birth, the rank and social influence of different relatives tends to carry greater weight than their actual relationship, and to be the deciding factor in determining the extent of their influence on the younger generation."[23]

At about the age of eight or nine boys and girls are ex-truded from the parental home "and go to sleep in separate quarters."[24]

The *Bushmen*, nomadic hunters and gatherers of South Africa, are organized into bands; the heads of the constitu-ent families of the band are usually male relatives of the chief. Descent is patrilineal. For the first three or four years of life, children are brought up almost exclusively by their mothers. After that, boys join the company of their fathers and are taught by them, by their grandfathers, and their uncles;[25] girls are entrusted to the care of older women, usu-ally their grandmothers.[26] A short time later, both boys and girls sleep separately from their parents. Boys sleep either in huts erected for them or in the open, under a tree in the center of the camp. Girls go to live in the hut for unmarried women.[27]

The *Chagga* of northeast Tanganyika are aligned sociologically in patrilocal extended families and patrilineal clans. The most important persons in the education of the child, in addition to his parents, are his grandparents, uncles, and aunts, with the heaviest emphasis on the paternal side.[28] Extrusion is practiced only for boys; the eldest and youngest sons are sent to the paternal grandparents, while the others are sent to the maternal grandparents.[29]

The *Dahomeans* of West Africa are organized sociologically into patrilocal extended families, patrilineal clans, social classes, and mutual-aid societies. Each extended family occupies its own compound of houses, and it is within this patrilineal context that children are reared and socialized rather than exclusively within their parents' nuclear families.[30] Marriage is polygynous, the husband spending allotted times in the hut of each wife, and each woman keeps her younger offspring with her in her hut. "The boys at the age of nine or ten no longer sleep in the houses of their mothers. In a given compound or collectivity, all the boys of this age form a group, and build a house."[31] Girls at about the age of nine or ten may remain with their mothers, but more often go to sleep at night in the homes of their paternal grandmothers.

The *Gros Ventres* of Montana were buffalo hunters in their aboriginal lives on the Canadian Plains. The principal social grouping of the Gros Ventres was the patrilineal band; residence upon marriage was patrilocal. Children were brought up by their parents as well as by their fathers' sisters, who had specific duties in the upbringing of their nephews and nieces, especially in disciplinary matters and in teaching etiquette; the maternal uncle also had the right to reprimand his sister's children.[32]

A Gros Ventres girl "was removed from her own family at an early age and was brought up in a different household."[33] Boys continued to reside with their parents until they joined the age-graded "companies" of warriors at about the age of sixteen or seventeen, but the extrusion of the girls provided the basis for brother-sister avoidance. "If it could possibly be avoided, brother and sister did not speak to nor look directly at each other. They communicated through a third person."[34]

The *Hopi* of northeast Arizona are sedentary agriculturalists who reside in permanent villages. They are organized sociologically into matrilocal extended families and matrilineal lineages and clans. Much of Hopi culture is focused on religious ritual and observances which are largely concentrated in the *kiva*, the subterranean ceremonial structure. Children are brought up by their parents as well as by kinsmen of both sides, but some of the most significant learning takes place with matrilineal kin.[35] "In the old days, at least, training for subsistence came primarily from the 'fathers,' aided by the 'grandfathers,' and ritual training came largely from the 'mother's brothers' in the case of the boy. For a girl both economic and ritual training comes primarily from her 'mothers' and mother's mother, with some aid from the 'mother's brothers.' "[36]

At about the age of eight or ten years, children of both sexes are introduced to the major religious institutions of Hopi society, the *Katcina* cult, and boys are extruded from the household; girls are not extruded. "In summer, boys often sleep out of doors, either on the roof or near the building. In winter, they sleep in a storage room, which may be some distance from the house, or in a *kiva*. A number of boys usually sleep together."[37]

The *Jukun*-speaking people of Nigeria are sedentary and agricultural. Traditionally, the Jukun have been matrilineal, organized sociologically into matrilocal extended families and matrilineal lineages. More recently, under the influence of British rule, the Jukun have been veering toward a patrilineal system, and the juxtaposition of the two rules of descent seem to be leading toward a bilateral system. Our present discussion of the Jukun will deal with them as of their matrilineal state.

Throughout childhood, a child's maternal uncle was one of the most dominant and significant educative influences; "a Jukun, in fact, fears his maternal uncle more than his father or any paternal uncle; for he regards his maternal uncle as his lord and master."[38] Marriage among the Jukun was polygynous, a man sharing a hut with each wife in rotation; when a man spent a night with his wife, her children were often sent to sleep in the huts of her co-wives.[39] At about the age of nine, boys went to live with their maternal uncles and remained there until marriage, when they returned to their parents' home.[40]

The *Kurtatchi*, of the island of Bougainville in Melanesia, are organized sociologically into matrilineal clans; they are a sedentary and agricultural people. A Kurtatchi child not only comes under the influence of his parents in the course of growing up, but is also subjected to the education and discipline of his maternal uncle.[41] "The first group of people with which our Melanesian child will learn to associate himself officially consists of his mother and all her siblings, his mother's mother, if she be living, his own full brothers and sisters, and the children of all the women just mentioned, but not those of the men; in other words, those of his blood relations who are of the same clan, the clan always passing through the mother."[42] With respect to discipline, "the child . . . will be taught from his infancy to regard as the person having the most authority over him his mother's eldest brother. . . . [And] this man is himself under the authority of his own mother's eldest living brother, as long as any survive."[43]

At about eight or nine years of age, boys go through the first two of a series of ceremonies marking their transition from childhood.[44] The first of these is their extrusion from their parents' homes to a hut or a house set aside for the use of the boys and other unmarried males. The second of the ceremonies at this stage consists of donning an unusual headgear (called *upi*) which is their mark, setting them off from those who are younger as well as from those who have completed all their initiation ceremonies. "Boys wearing the *upi* may not go into any house where a woman lives, even their own mother's. Their female relatives may prepare their food, but it must be handed out to them through the door at the *tagoan* (men's veranda). A boy breaking this rule would, in the olden days, have been killed, and his body eaten by the older men. Now they would 'make poison' against him and his father and mother, so that all three would die. This taboo on entering a woman's hut is still most meticulously kept."[45] At the time that boys put on the *upi*, the mothers display much "grief, which is probably not only ritual but real, for the putting on of the *upi* makes a break in the family circle."[46]

At about the same age, girls are also extruded; a girl is sent to the village and the home of the youth to whom she has been betrothed, remaining in the hut of her prospective husband's mother. "The girl stays . . . with her [future] hus-band's mother, who must keep her however bitterly she may cry."[47]

The *Kwoma* of New Guinea are a sedentary agricultural people who are organized sociologically into patrilineal lineages. Until the age of about eight or nine, children are brought up principally by their parents. From the descriptions of household compositions among the Kwoma,[48] it seems fairly clear that boys are extruded to the homes of their fathers' brothers at about the age of eight or nine and are brought up by these kinsmen thenceforward. It does not appear that girls are extruded.

The *Lamba* of northern Rhodesia are sedentary agriculturalists who supplement their diet by hunting. They are organized sociologically into matrilineal clans. A father's formal duties with respect to his offspring consist of providing food and clothing; teaching a child is primarily the responsibility of his mother, his maternal uncle, and his maternal grandmother.[49]

A child among the Lamba is subjected to two extrusions. The first occurs in early childhood when he goes to live in the hut of his maternal grandmother, at about five years of age, though it sometimes takes place earlier.[50] The second extrusion occurs a few years later when the boys (and, apparently, the girls as well) build their miniature huts on the outskirts of the village "and where they reign supreme."[51]

The *Lesu*, of the island of the same name in New Ireland in Melanesia, are organized sociologically into matrilineal clans and subsist by agriculture and fishing; they are a sedentary people. Children come under the educative influences of their parents plus the women who are members of their mother's clan; the maternal uncle is not involved in the upbringing of his sister's children.[52] "The unmarried men and the boys after the age of nine or ten, sleep in the men's house. There is no girl's house corresponding to the men's house, and the girls sleep at home until they are married."[53] During the day, however, boys eat in their parents' households and participate in the affairs of that group.

The *Malekula* of the New Hebrides Islands are a sedantary people who are organized into localized patrilineal clans. Children, especially boys, are brought up by their parents plus patrilineal kinsmen.[54] At the edge of every village is a club-house for men, and it is here that boys sleep when they are extruded from the parental household.[55] Within the club-house are partitions dividing the house into compartments, each of which is occupied by an age-grade; "within each is an oven or fireplace, at which members of the grade occupying that compartment cook their food."[56] It is taboo for a boy or man to eat in any compartment but his own.

The *Manuans* of Samoa are organized sociologically into exogamous bilateral kin groups which take on many of the characteristics of unilinear descent groups, especially in the ownership and control of land. "The only institutionalized contacts of young children are with the members of their descent groups and their households."[57] One of the outstanding features of the Manuan pattern of child-rearing is the rule that "any older relative has a right to demand personal service from younger relatives, a right to criticise their conduct and to interfere in their affairs . . . . For the children an hour's escape from surveillance is almost impossible."[58] Although there appear to be resulting negative feelings toward most kinsmen as a result, a child's "attitude to his paternal aunt or great-aunt is more heavily tinged with fear."[59]

The Manuans do not practice extrusion, although there is a decided tendency for young unmarried males to sleep in their friends' houses or in empty guest houses.[60] They do, however, practice brother-sister avoidance; "those who call each other brother and sister cannot talk together, eat together, walk together, touch each other, use each other's possessions, dance on the same dance floor, travel together, nor take part in the same small group festivities."[61] This taboo or avoidance begins at about the age of nine or ten; "after marriage it takes on more of an attitude of respect and fear."[62]

The *Murngin*, nomadic hunters and gatherers of northern Australia, are organized into a variety of social groupings, the most significant of which are the band and the patrilineal clan. "A father never corrects his children,"[63] and "a mother seldom corrects her child."[64] These educative functions are left to other kinsmen within the band. Religious and sacred knowledge is also acquired from older patrilineal kin.[65] Somewhere between the ages of six and eight, a Murngin boy undergoes three experiences: he is extruded from his family, he is subjected to brother-sister avoidance, and he is circumcised.[66]

The *Navaho* of Arizona and New Mexico are sedentary pastoralists who are aligned sociologically into matrilocal extended families and matrilineal clans which are not localized. The upbringing of Navaho children shades off from the family into the clan, and child-rearing can be said to be shared by the family and the clan of which it is a part. For example, "the relationship of maternal uncles to their nephews and nieces was of great importance. These uncles assumed many of the disciplinary and instructional functions which fall to the lot of the father in white society."[67] Discipline, especially, is a process which is handled by people outside the child's family, and "the overwhelming tendency is to refer discipline, and the authority for it, to some individual or agency outside the immediate family circle. Neither parents nor grandparents nor older brothers or sisters habitually assume full responsibility in the eyes of the child."[68]

Every Navaho household or establishment consists of several structures, the basic units of which are the *hogans*, the living quarters. As the number of children increases in a family, and as they grow older, the family will build an extra *hogan* "where the boys sleep."[69] Girls are apparently not extruded.

The *Papago* of Arizona and adjacent Mexico were organized sociologically in their aboriginal state into patrilocal extended families and localized patrilineal clans. They were sedentary and agricultural. Very early in a child's life he came under the educative influence of his paternal grandmother, who shared almost equal responsibility with the mother in rearing the child, and other adult relatives such as uncles and aunts also played a large role in his socialization.[70] "From the beginning the child is strongly aware that these people are relatives. He is taught to use the proper kinship terms and slowly comes to see the lines of authority in the household."[71] Later on, the grandfather assumes the major responsibility in rearing the boy, and the girl remains under the tutelage of her grandmother.[72] Children continue to sleep with the parents until they are nine or ten years old, at which time they are sent to sleep with their grandparents.[73]

The *Pukapukans* of east central Polynesia are aligned sociologically into a combination of matrilineal and patrilineal descent groups, but the matrilineal lineage appears to be dying out and patrilineal descent seems to be in the process of becoming dominant. They are a sedentary people, subsisting primarily on agriculture. The education of children was carried out as much outside the home as within, and proceeded along sex-lines. Thus, "while the boy associates with his male elders and absorbs a knowledge of fish and fishing methods, the girl stays with her adult female relatives and learns the preparation of foods and the plaiting of baskets, food containers, mats and clothing."[74]

Children were ordinarily educated and reared by those kinsmen into whose homes they were extruded at an early age, although it does appear that a considerable number of children did not remain within the home of any one particular kinsmen but shifted their residences among these kin rather often.[75]

The *Tallensi,* of the northern Gold Coast, are organized sociologically into polygynous patrilocal extended families, patrilineal lineages and clans. The clan is a localized group, and the Tallensi are sedentary and agricultural. "Properly speaking it is only the father who exercises authority over a child; a mother rules her child through love and solicitude."[76] At the same time, however, paternal kin are intimately involved in a child's upbringing; "all those who are socially identifiable with one's parents and play a part in one's upbringing can, and in certain circumstances must, stand to one in the relation of proxy parents."[77] Kinsmen beyond the limits of the clan "are no longer concerned with the rearing of the child."[78]

At about the age of seven or eight, a boy is extruded from his mother's hut and goes to sleep either with a grandparent or, as is more frequently the case, in a hut of his own within his father's compound. "A boy ... is ridiculed by his playmates if he still sleeps in his mother's room after the age of seven or eight. . . . Tallensi are horrified at the suggestion that children who 'have sense' might witness sexual relations between their parents."[79] Girls continue to sleep in their mothers' rooms until they are married; except on those nights on which their fathers visit with their mothers.[80]

The *Tanala*, a Malayo-Polynesian people of Madagascar, are organized into patrilocal extended families, patrilineal lineages and clans; they live in permanent villages. Every man brings up two generations of children, his own and those of his sons; reciprocally, every child is brought up by his father and his father's father.[81] Every establishment has a separate dwelling, known as the "children's house," to which the boys are extruded; they sleep there at night, but participate in the family's activities and eat with the family during the day. "All the children of a family use the house in common, but the eldest son has a prior right. When the eldest son marries, he usually takes his house as his dwelling and a new one is built for the remaining children."[82]

The *Thonga* of southern Mozambique are sedentary

farmers who live in patrilocal extended families, patrilineal lineages and clans. Discipline over children is exercised more by patrilineal kinsmen, especially the paternal grandfather, than by parents.[83] "The maternal grandfather is. . . respected for his age. He is however more lenient to his grandson by his daughter than to his grandson by his son. If the first damages anything, he will say: 'That is no business of mine. . . . ' But if it were his grandson by his son, it would be a totally different matter, and he would be hard on him."[84] Extrusion is practiced for both boys and girls. Two huts, one for each sex, are erected on either side of the entrance to the parental hut.[85]

The *Tikopia*, of the island of the same name in the Solomons, in Polynesia, are primarily agriculturalists residing in permanent villages. They are grouped in patrilocal extended families, patrilineal lineages and four patrilineal clans. The rearing of a child is not only the concern of his parents, but "the kinship factor in education is extremely important, and by the natives themselves it is continually stressed."[86] A wide range of paternal kinsmen — in addition to maternal kinsmen — perform a variety of educative functions with respect to any one child. Thus, "the actual care of the child, the feeding of it, carrying of it, issuing commands to it, punishing it and educating it is performed in different cases, partially at least by different sets of relatives."[87] Clansmen teach etiquette and lore to each other's children, but the emphasis is on discipline; a child's "father, his father's brothers and cousins reprove him as they do each other's children,[88] and "children are kept in control by the near relatives of their parents as well as by these latter."[89] This, of course, is reflected in the reciprocal behavior

[86]

of children toward their kinsmen; "as far as the modified obligations are concerned, it is difficult to see any difference between the way in which a boy treats his own father and that in which he treats his father's brothers."[90]

The Tikopia practice extrusion with respect to their young sons. "The behavior of a child in the family is apt to be influenced considerably by mechanisms which detach it from its parents and attach it to other members of the wider kinship groups."[91] One of these mechanisms is the custom whereby a young child, apparently around the age of eight or nine, is taken to live in the home of a distant kinsman; the child keeps his rights, privileges and titles in his parental home and visits his parents regularly, bringing gifts of food.[92]

The *Trobrianders* of Melanesia are sedentary horticulturalists who live in permanent villages and who are organized sociologically into matrilineal lineages and clans. "The mother's brother is considered the real guardian of a boy, and there is a series of mutual duties and obligations, which establish a very close and important relation between the two."[93] Brother-sister avoidance is established for Trobriand children at a relatively early age,[94] and, at about the same time, boys move into a bachelors' hut[95] They move into this hut either in the village of the mother's brother or in the village in which they were born. "The sons, as long as they remain in the same village, always eat in the parental house; the daughters remain at home till marriage."[96]

The following are the societies of the sample in which children are brought up for sociological independence:

The *Alorese*, of the island of Alor in the Netherlands

East Indies, are an agricultural people who reside in permanent villages. Descent is patrilineal, and the Alorese possess lineages; these groupings, however, do not function as cohesive institutions. Alorese children are brought up by their parents. Growing up in Alor is not a very pleasant experience, and children learn that when they are in difficulty some kinsman will offer them sanctuary; "just as children learn quickly enough to play one parent off against the other, so also they learn which kin will stand up for them when parental demands seem oppressive."[97] However, there are no kinsmen outside the family who have prescribed duties with respect to a child. Alorese children continue to live with their parents until marriage, and there are no avoidances imposed on brothers and sisters.

The Balinese of the Malay Archipelago are agriculturalists who reside in permanent villages; kinship is reckoned bilaterally. Children are brought up by their parents within the independent nuclear family.[98] Balinese children continue to live with their parents until they are married and do not practice brother-sister avoidance.

The Camayurá of northern Matto Grosso, Brazil, are semi-nomadic agriculturalists who move from one area to another as the soil becomes exhausted; kinship is reckoned bilaterally. Children are brought up by their parents, and although they are supposed to show the same respect toward their parents' siblings, the latter do not participate in rearing their nephews and nieces unless they are orphaned.[99] "Infants sleep with their mothers, but grown children have their hammocks slung near those of their parents."[100]

Cañamelar is a sugar plantation on the southern coast of Puerto Rico, and its inhabitants are wage-earners. Kinship is reckoned bilaterally. "The family is the most important single social institution in the lives of the people."[101] Children are brought up principally by their parents, although they do come under the influence of a variety of friends, relatives, school teachers and god-parents; but there are no kinsmen outside the family who have specific educative functions with respect to a child.[102] Children remain with the family until they become wage-earners.[103]

The *Chamorros* of the island of Guam are currently grouped into extended family groups and village communities. Matrilineal descent has been abolished under American rule, and matrilocal residence is disappearing. The dominant influence in the life of a child is his mother,[104] and as a result of the fact that "attendance of all children in the public schools is compulsory, . . . the young people are beginning to break away from strict parental discipline."[105] Kinsmen outside the family have no prescribed duties with respect to the socialization of a child; "usually a child has no recourse to his grandparents or other relatives and there is no one to rescue him from the anger of a parent or a guardian."[106] Children remain with their parents until they leave for wage-earning occupations or until marriage.

The *Chenchu* live in Hyderabad, in the Deccan of India. They are primarily hunters and gatherers, supplementing their diet with a small amount of millet, tomatoes, and chilis which they cultivate. Descent is counted bilaterally. With respect to rearing children, the nuclear family is an independent unit and the upbringing of children is entirely in the hands of parents.[107] Children continue to live with their parents until marriage.

Chimaltenango is a *municipio* in the Republic of Guatemala. The Indians of Chimaltenango are sedentary farmers who are organized into patrilineal kin groups which resemble lineages; the latter groups are made up of patrilocal extended families. The socialization of children in Chimaltenango is carried out principally within the bounds of the "patriarchal family."[108] Although "most of the adults with whom a child has contact during his first few years, except for occasional visits from the mother's relatives, are patrilineal kin,"[109] the latter do not appear to have any pre-scribed functions in rearing their nephews. Children continue to live in their parents' homes until marriage.[110]

The *Dusun* of north Borneo reside in self-sufficient agricultural communities; descent among them is reckoned bilaterally. Children come under the exclusive jurisdiction of their parents and remain within the same household as their parents until marriage.[111]

The *Copper Eskimo* of north central Canada are hunters and fishermen who reside in semi-permanent settlements. Descent is counted bilaterally. Eskimo children are brought up within the confines of the independent nuclear family and persons outside this group appear wholly uninvolved in the upbringing of the young.[112] Children remain in the homes of their parents until marriage.[113]

The *Fijians* of Polynesia are sedentary agriculturalists who reside in permanent villages. Descent is reckoned matrilineally, but there are no small kin groups that function as corporate units. In addition to being brought up within the family, boys around the age of ten or eleven tend to attach themselves to an older man and serve him by running errands or by helping him in different ways; but there does not appear to be any rule as to whether such a man must be a kinsman.[114] Children continue to live at home until marriage.

The *Ifaluk* of the Caroline Islands in Micronesia, who are agriculturalists and fishermen, trace their descent matrilineally and are grouped into matrilocal extended families, matrilineal lineages and matrilineal clans. In former times, a child's mother's brother played a great role in his upbringing, but today this emphasis is gradually tending to disappear.[115] Also in former times, the Ifaluk used to practice extrusion and brother-sister avoidance, but these customs too, have died out; "now that the men's houses are no longer used as bachelors' dormitories, and the young men sleep in their own homesteads, an unmarried man and his sister often sleep in the same dwelling."[116]

The *Kaingang*, nomadic hunting and gathering Indians of southeastern Brazil, are grouped into bands of from fifty to three hundred people. These bands are further subdivided into smaller units of from two to twenty persons who wander from place to place. The Kaingang trace their descent patrilineally, but there is a "very lack of fixity of relationships"[117] in their social system. Children are brought up by their parents and remain with their parents until they marry; nor is there any pattern of brother-sister avoidance.[118]

The *Kaska* Indians reside in British Columbia and in the southern Yukon, west of the Rocky Mountains. The Kaska are semi-nomadic hunters, gatherers and fishermen. Kinship is reckoned matrilineally. Children are brought up almost entirely within the confines of the independent nuclear family; "discipline is restricted to the family and is rarely shared by other adults."[119] Formal schooling by strangers or non-relatives is beginning to play a role in the upbringing of a

Kaska child; "most of the parents are ready to send their children to summer mission school and, at least in early years, try to insist on such attendance."[120] There are no avoidances prescribed for brothers and sisters.[121]

The *Kwakiutl* of British Columbia are sedentary fishermen who supplement their diet by gathering; they practice little or no agriculture. They trace their descent patrilineally, and are organized sociologically into clans which are usually localized. Children are brought up within the bounds of the nuclear family,[122] and remain within the family until marriage.[123]

The *Lakher* of Assam in eastern India are a sedentary people who are aligned sociologically into patrilineal clans. Children are brought up by their parents plus maternal uncles, but patrilineal kin outside the family appear not to be involved in a child's socialization. "It is very difficult to say whether . . . the maternal uncle and his wife, or a person's parents come next in order of respect; some people give preference to the maternal uncle and some to the parents. Looked at from certain points of view, the maternal uncle has a position of authority; looked at from others, the parents are more important."[124] At about the age of nine, boys are extruded and go to sleep with other young men and boys or, later, in the home of girls whom they are courting.[125]

The *Lepcha* of Sikkim in the Himalayan Mountains are sedentary agriculturalists who are aligned sociologically into patrilocal extended families and patrilineal clans. Children are brought up almost exclusively by their parents[126] and remain with their parents until marriage.[127]

The *Marquesans* of eastern Polynesia are sedentary farmers and fishermen. They reckon their descent bilaterally and
they practiced polyandrous marriage. "The rearing of children was largely in the hands of men,"[128] that is, the child's
mother's husbands, who were not members of the child's descent group. Maternal kinsmen confined their participation
in the life of a child to sponsoring him in the elaborate net-
work of social ranking.[129] Children continued to live in
their parents' homes until marriage; there was a separate
dwelling for men only, but it was reserved for old men past
senescence "and young men could enter only after a considerable period of sexual abstinence."[130]

The *Midlanders* of North America (my designation for
contemporary American mid-westerners) are generally sedentary entrepeneurs and wage-workers residing in permanent
settlements of varying sizes. Descent among them is reckoned bilaterally. Children are brought up by their parents
within the bounds of the independent nuclear family as well
as by non-kin in formally age-graded schools.[131] Children
generally continue to live at home until marriage, and brothers and sisters sometimes share the same room for
sleeping.[132]

Mirebalais is a commune in central Haiti which is inhab-
ited by peasant farmers who reside in a permanent village.
Descent in Mirebalais is bilateral. Children are brought up
by their parents within the independent nuclear family and
generally continue to live with their parents until marriage.[133]

Moche is a community near the coast of Peru; the
Mocheros are sedentary and independent farmers who reck-

on their kinship bilaterally. Children are brought up within the bounds of the independent nuclear family.[134] Children remain within the family until marriage.[135]

The *Nama* Hottentots of southeastern Africa are nomadic pastoralists who trace their descent patrilineally; they are organized into patrilineal clans. Children are brought up by their parents plus their maternal uncles, but not by patrilineal kin.[136] "Each family had its own hut, where the children remain with their parents till marriage."[137]

The *Ojibwa* Indians of northernmost Wisconsin and southwest Ontario are hunters and gatherers who live in an environment of considerable scarcity. During the winter each nuclear family is completely isolated from all others in order to make the most of a meager supply of food; families come together during the summer, but even here the theme of familial isolation predominates. The Ojibwa reckon their descent patrilineally, but there are no kin groups outside the family, and patrilineal descent functions only in regulating marriage. "Politically and economically the Ojibwa are an atomistic society. Functionally, the household is the irreducible unit; but in the cultural thought, the individual person is the unit."[138] Concomitantly, the rules of Ojibwa society restrict the upbringing of children to the isolated and independent nuclear family. "It is incumbent upon the father (or stepfather) to punish the child's wrong-doings, but no one else has the right."[139] The confinement of child-rearing to the nuclear family obtains even in instances of polygynous marriage; "the Ojibwa practice polygyny not that several wives may cooperate to enrich the household, but because the husband is clever enough as hunter and medicine man to provide for his several wives and their children. . . . Though all may live under one roof, each wife and her children have a separate apartment, and each apartment operates as an independent household."[140]

Okinawa is the largest island in the Ryukyu Archipelago in the Western Pacific. The Okinawans reported on here[141] are entirely agriculturalists and reside in permanent villages. The sociological groupings of the Okinawans are patrilocal extended families and patrilineal clans which crosscut the entire island. The education of children is carried out within the family and at schools which are conducted by non-kinsmen. Children remain within the parental household until marriage, and there are no customs prescribing brother-sister avoidance.

The *Omaha*, Plains Indians of Iowa and Nebraska, were primarily buffalo hunters in their aboriginal state. Kinship was traced patrilineally, and kinsmen were grouped sociologically into patrilineal clans, the primary function of which was the regulation of marriage by clan exogamy. Rearing children was in the hands of the independent nuclear family and the maternal uncle; patrilineal kin outside the family were not involved in a child's upbringing.[142] Brother-sister avoidance was absent from this Plains tribe and children continued to live in the parental household until marriage.[143]

Rocky Roads is a community in the central mountains of Jamaica, of sedentary peasant farmers who trace their descent bilaterally. Children are brought up exclusively within the isolated and independent nuclear family as well as in schools conducted by strangers.[144] Children remain within the family until marriage or until they leave the community to find wage-work on plantations or in towns; there are no patterns of avoidance between siblings of the opposite sex,[145] who often sleep in the same room.

The *Sanpoil*, Salishan Indians residing on the Columbia River in eastern Washington, live in permanent village settlements; subsistence is by means of fishing, hunting, and gathering. Kinship is reckoned bilaterally. Children were brought up by their parents, but corporal punishment was carried out by "the old man from up the river," a non-kinsman who appeared in disguise and whipped misbehaving children ritually.[146] Children remain at home until marriage, although boys do an extensive amount of traveling during adolescence.[147]

The *Shtetl*, a term encompassing the socially isolated communities of Jews in eastern Europe prior to the Second World War, was composed of sedentary horticulturalists, entrepreneurs, and hierarchies of religious functionaries. Descent was reckoned bilaterally. Children were brought up within the confines of the nuclear family, the mother predominating in the socialization process, as well as by non-related teachers in school.[148] Children were often sent away to school but returned home on vacations and slept in their parents' homes during these times; nor was brother-sister avoidance practiced.[149]

The *Sirionó* of eastern Bolivia are nomadic hunters and gatherers who travel in bands generally composed of matrilineally related persons. The upbringing of children is primarily the responsibility of parents; "in contrast to many primitive societies, where a maternal or paternal relative often assumes the responsibility of formally educating the child, the system of education among the Sirionó may best be characterized as informal, random, and haphazard."[150] Children remain with their parents until marriage, which occurs at a very early age. "A certain reserve can also be noted in the relationships between siblings of the opposite sex; this never reaches the point of avoidance, however."[151]

The *Slave,* of Fort Nelson, Canada, were, in their aboriginal state, nomadic hunters and gatherers who moved about in small bands. Descent was counted bilaterally. "The socialization of the growing child was closely centered within the immediate family, with parents as the most important teachers. A child who lacked a family was apparently not faced with a happy lot."[152] Children remained with their families until marriage.

Suye Mura is a peasant village on the main Japanese island of Honshu. Kinship is reckoned patrilineally. The education of children takes place in the home and in school.[153] There is neither extrusion nor brother-sister avoidance among the people of Suye Mura.

Taitou is a village in Shantung Province, China. The people of Taitou are peasant farmers who are divided into four patrilineal clans, each of which tends to form one of the four divisions of the village. Kinship is reckoned patrilineally and residence upon marriage is patrilocal. Children are brought up within the family and at school. The father's brother has the right to punish a boy only if the former is unmarried; after his marriage he has no rights in rearing a nephew.[154] Children remain at home until marriage and there is no brother-sister avoidance.[155]

The *Tarascans* of Mexico, who trace their descent bilaterally, are sedentary peasant farmers. Children are brought up by their parents, god-parents, and sometimes at school.[156] They remain with their parents until marriage, and there is no pattern of brother-sister avoidance.[157]

The *Teton Dakota* are a Sioux Indian tribe of South Dakota who have been living a sedentary life on a reservation since the latter part of the nineteenth century. Descent among them is counted bilaterally. Children are brought up at home, especially by their mothers, and at school.[158] Children remain at home until they are married or until they leave to find employment, and the aboriginal patterns of brother-sister avoidance have completely disappeared.[159]

The *Witoto* are an Amazonian tribe in Brazil and Colombia. They are a semi-nomadic people who practice slash-and-burn agriculture, and they are also hunters and fishermen. They are aligned sociologically into patrilocal extended families and patrilineal clans. Children are brought up within the bounds of the nuclear family, boys coming under the authority of their fathers and girls under that of their mothers.[160] Children continue to live with their parents until marriage and brother-sister avoidance appears to be absent.[161]

The *Yakut* of northeastern Siberia are semi-nomadic pastoralists who live in a rather forbidding and impoverished environment. They trace their descent patrilineally, and they are organized into patrilocal extended families and patrilineal clans. Children are brought up within the confines of the nuclear family and continue to live in the homes of their parents until they are married.[162]

The *Yurok* Indians are hunters, fishermen, and gatherers who live near the Pacific Ocean in extreme northern California. Residence is in permanent villages; descent is generally reckoned patrilineally. Yurok children are brought up almost exclusively within the confines of the independent nuclear family. Although boys generally join a sweat-house at about puberty, such membership is not prescribed, nor is brother-sister avoidance.[163]

The *Zadruga* of Croatia was a self-sustaining social and economic unit which held its land in common. Descent was reckoned bilaterally. Children were brought up almost exclusively by their parents, and neither extrusion nor brother-sister avoidance was practiced.[164]

FIVE

CEREMONIES OF THE SECOND
STAGE OF PUBERTY:
INITIATION CEREMONIES

T HE second stage of puber-
ty begins with the appearance of the observable secondary
sex characteristics. This appearance is the physiological manifestation of the biochemical and hormonal changes which
constituted the basis of the first stage of puberty. Of course
the physiological states which commence at the latter stage
of development continue for many years beyond their initiation.

I suggested earlier that the second stage of puberty would
be less confusing to the child than the first stage. Naturally,
new problems are presented to the individual: an adolescent is confronted with a new "body image" and with physical and emotional problems that vary among societies. Often, a re-evaluation of customary modes of getting along with
people takes place. But whatever the uncertainties and confusion of this period, they are less than the vulnerability and
precariousness of the first stage, because of the observabil-
ity of the changes that are taking place.*

*American as well as other societies exacerbate the confusions and vulnera-
bilities of the second stage to the point of the classical "adolescent conflict." This, however, is unusual when viewed cross-culturally and it would
also appear to be an exaggeration of the underlying biological processes.

Ceremonies of the Second Stage of Puberty

It is for this reason that I hypothesized that fewer societies would take formal, explicit and institutionalized steps in connection with the second stage than with the first, and that whatever steps *are* taken at the second stage of puberty will be less drastic than those related to the first. Specifically, the initiation ceremonies that often take place at about the time of the second stage of puberty will occur in fewer societies than practice extrusion or brother-sister avoidance, and these ceremonies are much less drastic in their effects than either extrusion or brother-sister avoidance.

Why is so much attention given to the *rites de passage* of the second stage, when in fact they are of less importance than the more neglected events of the first stage? The former are usually surrounded by pageantry and pomp. They are colorful and often mobilize the energies of many people at once, and at their apogees are often accompanied by the pained cries of initiates and the wails of their mothers and sisters. On the other hand, the simple act of extrusion or the imposition of the rule of brother-sister avoidance seems drab and prosaic by comparison.

However, this holds only from the point of view of the observer. If we put ourselves in the place of the children who are being extruded or who are subjected to the rules of brother-sister avoidance, these two customs take on new dimensions and significance. Such words as drama, pageantry, color, and the like, are insipid to portray the impact of extrusion or brother-sister avoidance on an eight- or ten-year old child. The vividness and pain of the initiation rites are surely important, and they will be discussed at length; but it should be remembered that the customs of the first stage of puberty — extrusion and brother-sister avoidance — are more significant for the individual and for the society.

What are the special characteristics of an initiation ceremony? Van Gennep suggested the following: 1) The rite must be presided over by elders; 2) it involves a process of indoctrination into the customary practices of the group; and 3) it involves physical ordeals, such as circumcision, or some other form of genital mutilation, or scarification.[1]

These characteristics are at the core of initiation ceremonies, but they are insufficient as a set of distinguishing features because they refer to too many different kinds of rites. From the point of view of the individual's relationships to social groups and his anchorage in them, it is necessary to distinguish between ceremonies that center on the individual child and those that center on a group. Thus, the ceremonies of the second stage with which I shall deal not only have the characteristics observed by Van Gennep but also the following four:

4) The rite is conducted by elders who are usually older members of the child's descent group and were involved in his upbringing; parents are usually excluded from the rite.

5) The rite must be universal for the members of the sex for which it is prescribed. That is, if initiation rites are prescribed for the boys of a society, they must be held for *all* boys of the appropriate age, and similarly for girls.*

6) The rite must be conducted in a group and not focused on a single individual. If initiation at this stage of develop-

---

*For this reason, the custom of the debut in the upper classes of some Western countries is not a true initiation ceremony, as some sociologists have tried to suggest (see, for example, Bossard and Boll 1948). This custom is usually restricted to loose socio-economic sub-groups within the society; there are no rules in the society at large which exclude a girl from adolescent or adult status if she does not go through the ceremony of the debut, and the decision to hold the debut rests with the girl's family and with the girl herself.

[102]

ment is prescribed for boys, then it is a group of boys who are being initiated, and similarly for girls.†

7) The opposite sex is usually excluded from witnessing the rite, whether or not it includes genital mutilation or exposure. When boys are being initiated, all females, regardless of age or status, are usually forbidden to witness the proceedings. Often, in the case of the initiation of boys, the kinswomen of the initiates may stand in a group at a distance from the ceremony itself, and the mingling of the sounds of the ceremony with those of the women form a kind of long-distance communication.* Sometimes the initiates are forbidden to cry out, and their silence together with the cries of the women forms a similar communication; the nature of this communication will be discussed below.

The second stage of puberty is an outgrowth of the first, and there is continuity from one to the other. Thus, initiation ceremonies are sequentially related and otherwise similar to extrusion and brother-sister avoidance.

The customs of both the first and second stages of puberty have time limits set on them. Extrusion and brother-sister avoidance continue much longer than the initiation ceremonies of the second stage, but they are limited nevertheless: they usually last from the beginning of the first stage of puberty until marriage. Initiation rites may last a day, a week, a month, or four months, but rarely more. Often the initiates undergo ordeals, or mutilations of one sort

†For this reason, the Jewish ceremony of the *bar mitzvah*, the individual confirmation rite which takes place traditionally on a boy's thirteenth birthday and which admits him to the religious fellowship or sodality, is not a true *rite de passage*.

*This is often an extraordinarily important part of the initiation ceremonies, and I will discuss its key role in these rites.

or another, and these will extend the duration of the rites beyond a week. Much time may be devoted to preparations for these ordeals, or to instruction in religious, sexual, mythical, or historical lore and rules. Sometimes these ceremonies are the occasions for initiates to choose their "blood brothers" and are used for instruction in the etiquette and rules governing this kind of friendship.[2]

Perhaps the most important similarity between the two is a marked disjunction in normal social activities and relationships. This is one of the principal purposes of extrusion and brother-sister avoidance, and it is also one of the main functions of the initiation ceremonies of the second stage of puberty. The former impose sudden breaks in the child's ties to members of his nuclear family. The latter also disrupt meaningful relationships.

There occurs, of course, a relatively abrupt cessation of normal economic and play activities for the initiates; their daytime family activities also stop until after the ceremonies have been concluded. But more important, the children participating in the rituals are usually forbidden contact with any member of the opposite sex and often with their parent of the same sex. They are hurt, usually genitally, and death can occur; yet boys cannot turn to their mothers for protection or comfort, and girls cannot turn to their fathers. Almost any child in any culture — and most adults, too — would feel abandoned, rejected, vulnerable, and emotionally hurt under these circumstances. There is no more effective way to deflect a child's emotional dependence away from his nuclear family than to traumatize him and at the same time forbid him to turn to the well-established security and comfort of his family for protection.

This view of initiation ceremonies, as societal means for manipulating the child's relationships with his nuclear family, conforms closely to Young's finding that male initiation ceremonies are dramatizations of male solidarity:

> Although solidarity is a matter of degree, a crucial threshold develops when the men of a village come to see themselves as a consciously organized group with the power to exclude or discipline its membership. . . . In societies with a high degree of male solidarity, stabilization of sex roles is not complete until the boy identifies with the male group, since such identification is a major component of the sex role. . . . What could be more impressive to both the youth and the community than to be publicly subincised or to be the center of attention of a group of village men intent on beating him severely?[2a]

The interpretation of initiation ceremonies that I am suggesting also conforms closely to Judith Brown's finding that

> . . . female initiation rites will occur in those societies in which the young girl continues to reside in the home of her mother after marriage. The purpose of the rites appears to be an announcement of status change both to the initiate and to those around her, made necessary because she spends her adult life in the same setting as her childhood. . . . Such rites will not be celebrated in those societies in which the young girl will leave her home and move to that of her husband's family, or to a new home removed from both families. The move itself serves to emphasize the status change to the young girl, and those among whom she will live will think of her as an adult, never having known her as a child.[2b]

Very often, especially while the boys are undergoing mutilation during the ritual, there occurs a dialogue of wailing between the initiates in their secluded camp and their mothers and sisters in the distance. Unseen to each other, they are able to maintain effective communication — moving, in a way pathetic, and of extraordinary significance in conveying to the initiates one all-important fact: Cry as they may, their mothers and sisters answer, and yet are powerless to help. This is the true climax of the initiation ceremony; this profound but futile dialogue of wails and cries is the crisis of deflection of energies away from the family. Even if the boys are silent, there exists full communication between the family and the initiates. It conveys to the two groups their separateness; and with inexorable force implants the idea in the youths that their families are beyond reach.

I emphasize this point because of the tendency of many observers to view initiation ceremonies as social instruments that permit an older generation to dramatize its disciplinary control over the younger generation — or to vent its aggression on the youngsters, or destroy any proclivities for rebellion.[3] There are many difficulties with such a point of view, not the least of which is that while genital mutilation of youngsters may be aggressive and hostile from the point of view of some Westerners, there is no reason to assume that all people who practice such customs are similarly motivated. Hostility in our society is not necessarily hostility in others.

The view that one of the goals of an older generation is to break the proclivities for rebellion in a younger generation presumes that fatherhood invariably generates feelings of insecurity under all socio-cultural conditions, and that insecurity must be compensated for by aggression and harsh discipline. There are surely Western and non-Western fathers who are motivated in this fashion toward their children; but there are also Western and non-Western fathers who are not.

Another difficulty with such a point of view is that it cannot explain why some societies practice these rites and others do not. If these ceremonies are hostile or aggressive in intent, are we then to assume that initiation ceremonies are only practiced in societies in which the level of rivalry between generations is highest? Even if there were merit to this hypothesis, there is still the problem of measuring the level of hostility between the generations in alien societies. These matters clearly require further, systematic exploration.

While I do not wish to deny completely the possibility that initiation rituals serve as an adult method of disciplining youth, to treat them exclusively from this point of view fails to relate them to other institutional and value systems in the society. Hostilities, motivations, rivalries and envies are neither institutions nor values. Nothing in a social system exists in a vacuum, independent of other institutions and separate from the goals of the society. If these psychological tensions were truly the mainsprings of the transitional rituals, we would expect to find the latter in more societies than we do.

Paralleling the discontinuity in the child's relationships to his family in the initiation ceremonies of the second stage of puberty is a break in spatial relationships to his world of familiarity. Brother-sister avoidance involves physical distance and separation. Extrusion is physical removal and seclusion from the opposite sex for about one-third of the day. Initiation ceremonies are almost always carried out in a secluded place from which certain people who are meaningful to the child are excluded.

There are two ways of looking at the fact that initiation ceremonies are of much briefer duration than extrusion and brother-sister avoidance. The first is that non-industrialized societies — where such customs are uniquely found — cannot afford to dispense with the labor of their adolescents for long periods. Horticultural, fishing, and hunting-and-gathering societies need the labor of youths for the acquisition and production of food. Hence, initiation ceremonies could not last beyond three or four months, regardless of their importance. The second is that it is difficult to imagine how the much briefer ceremonies of the second stage — where they do occur — could have as much impact on the developing personality as do either extrusion or brother-sister avoidance, which occur earlier and last much longer.

In this second point of view I disregard, for the moment, society's needs in maintaining a steady labor force for the production of food; I am thinking now solely in terms of the effects of these experiences on the youngsters themselves. Pubescent children are still not mature enough to evaluate their experiences in the light of social requirements; they are still too bound up with themselves and with their own bodies, though much less so than earlier, to understand fully that one ceremony is briefer than others because their labor is indispensable. Thus, if they had also been extruded from the household a few years earlier, or if the rule of brother-sister avoidance had been imposed on them, the initiation ceremony would seem mild by comparison.

While initiation ceremonies differ from extrusion and brother-sister avoidance in degree rather than kind, they also have important consequences. They involve separation and isolation from the family, bodily — usually genital — mutilation of one sort or another, removal from one social position to another; and all of these occur at a time of some psychological vulnerability. These four facts about initiation ceremonies are at the core of the rites, and they enable us to understand why they exist in certain kinds of societies and not in others. Of the four, the element of mutilation provides the major key.

I have suggested that the eventful upheavals that take place within individuals during the transition from childhood to adolescence are "exploited" in many societies, and that the child is more vulnerable and impressionable during the confusing first stage of puberty than during the second. Logically, then, the steps taken in the social system to impart new values are likely to be less drastic at the second stage of puberty than at the first. In fact, we might even expect that in some societies the less important second stage would go entirely unmarked by special ceremonies, even where the sociological preconditions for their occurrence apparently exist.

These preconditions, as seen in Chapters 3 and 4, consist of the presence of unilineal descent groups in the society's institutional organization. It might be reasonably expected that we would find a value system requiring the individual's anchorage within a descent group in every society with a system of clans and lineages. This is not, in fact, the case; anthropologists do not know why some societies display such value systems and others do not. However, in a society in which the value system does pivot on the individual's anchorage within the wider kin group outside the family — on the value of sociological interdependence — certain consequences follow. People in that society must be brought up so that they will have socio-emotional anchorage in the kin group, and if this is to be achieved, they must be brought up by members of their descent group as well as by their parents. If the child's energies for identification are to be deflected away from the family, he must be subjected to extrusion or brother-sister avoidance, or both. So much — but no more — appears inevitable. Beyond this, initiation ceremonies appear in some societies that have the value of sociological interdependence, but not in others. That is, initiation ceremonies are found in societies in which individuals are anchored in the wider kin group, but not in all such societies. Hence, socio-emotional anchorage in the descent group — sociological interdependence — is a necessary but not sufficient precondition for initiation ceremonies.

An initiation ceremony, with its attendant physical pain and isolation from parents, demonstrates to the youngster that his nuclear family is no longer his sole protector, refuge, and security. Thus, these rites of the second stage of puberty sometimes but not always appear as cultural means — in addition to extrusion and brother-sister avoidance — for deflecting energies for emotional identification and a sense of anchorage from the family toward the larger kin group. But the pain of the initiation ceremony is, after all, imposed by kinsmen who are members of this larger group. It is understandable that these energies will be deflected away from the family, but how — and why — are they re-directed toward the kin group?

There are several parts to the answer to this question. The first — and perhaps the most instructive — once again comes from the findings of experimental biologists and psychologists who deal with "critical periods of development."

Scott observes in his review of animal experimentation:[4]

"All [the] evidence indicates that any sort of strong emotion, whether hunger, fear, pain, or loneliness, will speed up the process of socialization.... We may also conclude that the speed of formation of a social bond is dependent upon the degree of emotional arousal, irrespective of the nature of that arousal.... One of the factors that brings the critical period to a close may be the developing ability of the young ... to associate fear responses with particular stimuli.... Fear responses thus have the dual effect of facilitating the formation of the social bond during the critical period (along with other emotions) and of bringing the period to a close.... In short, it seems likely that the formation of a social attachment through contact and emotional arousal is a process that may take place throughout life, and that although it may take place more slowly outside of certain critical periods, the capacity for such an attachment is never completely lost.

Evidence is accumulating ... that given any kind of emotional arousal a young animal will become attached to any individual or object with which it is in contact for a sufficiently long time.... It should not be surprising that many kinds of emotional reactions contribute to a social relationship. The surprising thing is that emotions which we normally consider aversive should produce the same effect as those which appear to be rewarding. This apparent paradox is partially resolved by evidence that the positive effect of unpleasant emotions is normally limited to early infancy by the development of escape reactions. Nevertheless, this concept leads to the somewhat alarming conclusion that an animal (and perhaps a person) of any age, exposed to certain individuals or physical surroundings for any length of time, will inevitably become attached to them, the rapidity of the process being governed by the degree of emotional arousal assssociated with them."

It is readily apparent that the over-all process of emotional attachment, in its genesis and functioning, is much more complex among humans than among other animals. But the physiological basis for such attachments is made clear through experimentation with primates and lower animal forms.

The second part of the answer to the question posed above is to be found in the fact that the child's rearing has been shared by those very kinsmen who are also his initiators. Thus, the youngster has had many years in which to build emotional identification with these relatives within the boundary-maintaining system of the kin group. Such identifications cannot be lost; they can be weakened, re-directed, or strengthened, but they cannot be dissolved.

Perhaps it is even more important that the child is initiated in a very special group. His fellow initiates at this second stage of puberty are not only his age-mates and his peers, but many of them are his kinsmen, members of his own descent group. It is within the group to which many of these belong that he will be anchored when he becomes a fully adult member of his society, and it is with this group that he is compelled to participate in this great crisis in his life. Furthermore, as we shall observe, it is for some of the actions of these kinsmen that he will have to assume responsibility later on.

The trauma that is experienced during an initiation ceremony of the second stage of puberty is a shared one, an experience suffered in common with a group of peers and age-mates. (In extrusion, the child usually sleeps with other members of his age-group in a men's house or some other grouping. The fact that brother-sister avoidance is not a shared trauma might account for its relative rarity.) The experiences of mutilation and isolation with a group not only serve to cushion the shock but also produce an exceptionally strong bond among the initiates. Thus, it is very often from among this group that a young man chooses his "best friend" or his "blood brother." These are people who remain inseparable friends for the rest of their lives, and so important are these bonds that they are often sanctioned by law and religious dogma.[5]

To sum up, in a form parallel to my earlier hypotheses: *In those societies in which children are brought up to be anchored in the wider kin group — for sociological interdependence — they will be brought up and taught by members of their descent group as well as by their parents, and during the second stage of puberty there may be a further disruption in the child's relationship to his family in the form of an initiation ceremony.* Conversely, *in those societies in which children are brought up to be anchored in the nuclear family — for sociological independence — they will be brought up and taught by their parents, or by non-members of the child's descent group as well as by their parents, and during the second stage of puberty there will be no disruption in the child's relationship with his family.* However, *fewer societies will take formal and explicit steps in connection with the second stage of puberty than with the first.*

The data from the sample of societies used for this study, as seen in Tables 5 and 6, substantiate these hypotheses. Extrusion or brother-sister avoidance are found in all of the twenty-eight societies in which children are brought up to be anchored in the descent group; however, only eighteen (64%) have initiation ceremonies at the second stage. There are thirty-seven societies in which children are brought up to be anchored in the nuclear family; extrusion or brother-

Table 5

Relationships between Agents of Socialization and
Initiation Ceremonies at the Second Stage
of Puberty

	Initiation Ceremonies	No Initiation Ceremonies
Socialization by parents plus members of child's descent group	18	10
Socialization by parents plus non-members of child's descent group	1	36
$X^2 = 26.44$	$T = .64$	$p < .001$

Table 6

Relationships between the Structure of Descent
Groups and Initiation Ceremonies at
the Second Stage of Puberty

	Initiation Ceremonies	No Initiation Ceremonies
Unilinear descent groups	18	26
No unilinear descent groups	1	20
$X^2 = 8.47$	$T = .36$	$p < .01$

[114]

sister avoidance is practiced in only one (Lakher boys are extruded at about the age of nine), and absent in all the others. Similarly, only one of these societies has initiation ceremonies (the Sirionó, for girls but not for boys), and they are absent in all the rest.

The following are the societies of the sample in which children are brought up for sociological interdependence:

The *Andaman Islanders*. With the appearance of the secondary sex characteristics, boys undergo a scarification ceremony individually, not in groups.[6] They then go to live in a bachelors' hut, where they remain until marriage. Girls formerly went to live in a spinsters' hut until they were married, but this custom appears to have died out. Now they simply continue to live with their foster-parents until marriage.

The *Chiricahua Apache*. There is no ceremony for boys when the secondary sex characteristics appear; they begin a regimen of physical toughening and hardening at about the age of seven and are not permitted to join in raids until they are sufficiently mature, usually after the age of sixteen.[7] A quasi-religious rite is performed for a girl at the time of her first menstruation, but it is not performed for a group of girls; at the same time, however, the rite is mandatory for each girl if she is to be considered marriageable. "Before this physiological event and her puberty rite, she is called a girl; afterward the term 'woman' is applied to her."[8]

The *Arapesh*. With the appearance of the secondary sex characteristics, a boy is ready for his initiation ceremony, but these rites usually only occur about once every six or seven years, when twelve or fifteen boys are initiated at once. In addition to learning the secrets of his society, "there is a ritual segregation from the company of women, during which time the novice observes certain special food taboos, is incised, eats a sacrificial meal of the blood of the older men, and is shown various marvellous things."[9] A minor rite — in which her brothers participate — is performed for a girl individually when she reaches menarche. "This ceremony which officially ends a girl's childhood is of another order from a boy's initiation, although it has many elements in common with it. . . . But the boy passes from one way of life into another; before, he was a boy, now he is a man with a man's responsibilities and therefore he may share in the secrets of men. For a girl there is no such emphasis."[10]

The *Arunta*. For boys, a circumcision ceremony takes place after the appearance of the secondary sex characteristics. This ceremony is controlled by the older men of the group and women are excluded; normally, two boys are operated on at any one ceremony.[11] Part of this ceremony involves the revelation of the secrets of the bull-roarers to the initiates. A sub-incision ceremony is performed after the circumcision wound is fully healed; women are rigidly excluded from this ceremony, too. The final rite is the "fire ceremony," which takes place at an indefinite time later, and which includes the women of the group. In this ceremony, a group of young men have to defend themselves with branches against burning grass and sticks which the women throw at their heads; then, to demonstrate their prowess, they must lie down for several minutes on green boughs laid over an open fire. Later they must kneel for a brief moment in the coals of a small fire. At this point they are considered men of the society.

There are two rituals for women, but neither takes place in a group of age-mates. When a girl's breasts begin to appear, they are rubbed with fat and red ochre to stimulate their growth. Around the time of her menarche, her hymen is surgically and ritually ruptured.

The *Bantu* of North Kavirondo. After the secondary sex characteristics begin to appear, boys go through an elaborate *rite de passage*, the high point of which is a circumcision ceremony performed on a group, never individually. During these ceremonies, each boy chooses one ritual friend, and this relationship can never be broken. During the operation, the boy's father stands near him, encourages him to stand in a steady position, "at the same time admonishing the operator to be careful with his knife."[12] Women and children are permitted to watch from a distance, although there is a period of seclusion before the ceremony itself. "If a boy still has enough energy left [after his circumcision] he may run after the operator, beat him with a stick, and try to tear off his head-dress. If he succeeds in doing so, the operator must give him three chickens as a reward for his pluck."[13] After recuperating from the operation, the boys spend about three months in a seclusion-hut during which time they are instructed by older clansmen. There are no ceremonies for girls in connection with the appearance of the secondary sex characteristics.

The *Basuto*. *Rites de passage* took place for boys and for girls at the appearance of the secondary sex characteristics. Boys and girls were initiated separately, and about fifteen youngsters went through the ceremonies together. Each of the sexes had its own formal seclusion, instruction by elder kinsmen in tribal secrets and in sexual matters, and its own secret songs and practices. Boys were circumcised and girls had their hymens ruptured surgically. Today these customs are all but dead. "Many Basuto have accepted the opinion that initiation is retrograde if not definitely immoral and now oppose it as strongly as any missionary.... The only people who still support the institution are the old conservatives who are attached to their traditions and customs, or admire the virtues it inculcates."[14] Initiation ceremonies did not produce or provide any significant changes in behavior or in status.

The *Bena*. Although ceremonies are performed for both sexes "at the first manifestations of puberty,"[15] there are *rites de passage* for girls only. "As soon as a boy tells his elders that he has experienced a spontaneous ejaculation during sleep they consult a doctor from whom they obtain medicine for him to eat, and then he is driven down to the river by a crowd of men beating him with sticks."[16] He is also given instruction concerning sexual intercourse. Without this ritual, it is believed, a boy will lose his virility. No circumcision or other mutilation is performed on the boys. Girls, on the other hand, go through a true *rite de passage* at this stage, when their *labia minora* are cut off "to prevent them growing and blocking the entrance to the vagina."[17]

The *Bushmen*. It is not clear from the published data whether the ceremonies for both sexes at the appearance of the secondary sex characteristics are truly *rites de passage* or whether they are held for each child individually.[18]

The *Chagga*. There is neither extrusion nor any other *rite de passage* for girls, but there is a true initiation ceremony for boys, which coincides with the appearance of the secondary sex characteristics.[19]

The *Dahomeans*. With the appearance of the secondary sex characteristics, boys go through a lengthy program in religious instruction, climaxed by a group circumcision ceremony; those who participate in this *rite de passage* together "regard themselves as 'brothers by the same knife,' who must not, therefore, think evil of one another."[20] There is no comparable ceremony for girls.

The *Gros Ventres*. No *rites de passage* were performed for either sex at the appearance of the secondary sex characteristics.

The *Hopi*. With the appearance of the secondary sex characteristics boys and girls undergo a true *rite de passage* in which children are taught the religious secrets of Hopi society and in which they are whipped, often severely. After these ceremonies they have the right to participate in the religious ceremonials of their respective clans.[21]

The *Jukun*. There do not appear to be any *rites de passage* for girls. There is a circumcision ceremony for boys, which today is considered the affair of paternal kinsmen but which in the matrilineal past may have been the concern of the maternal kin.

The *Kurtatchi*. At about the time of the appearance of the secondary sex characteristics, boys go through a final *rite de passage* in which the *upi* (headgear) is removed. There are no mutilations involved in any of the rites, and there are no ceremonies performed for girls at this time.[22]

The *Kwoma*. About every five years, a group of boys whose secondary sex characteristics have appeared are initiated into the age-grade system of Kwoma society. The climax of this *rite de passage*, which is highly elaborate, comes with the scarification ceremony; "all the boys of the proper age are operated on at a single ceremony. Each boy, when his turn comes, lies on a sago spathe. While the father of his future wife holds his hands, a special operator incises two semicircular cuts above each nipple and rubs ashes into them to make a raised scar."[23] Girls go through a similar operation, the incision being made around the navel.

The *Lamba*. There are no ceremonies performed for boys at the appearance of the secondary sex characteristics; instead, this transition "is gradual and imperceptible."[24] There is a rite for a girl at her first menstruation, but it is an individual — not a group — ceremony and usually involves some instruction to the girl by the local midwife.[25]

The *Lesu*. There is an initiation ceremony for the boys which has, as part of its ritual, their circumcision, seclusion, instruction, and the like.[26] "The rites seem to center around the initiation of the boys to masculine society and not around the actual circumcision, which is but an excuse. Before, the cutting of the ear lobes served as the *raison d'être*."[27] There is no *rite de passage* for girls.

The *Malekula*. There is a true *rite de passage* for boys, consisting of circumcision (or sometimes incision) as well as seclusion. "When it has been decided to hold the circum-cision rites, the father of each candidate seeks out someone who will act as guardian to his boy during the period of seclusion. For this service the guardian will, on the completion of the rites, receive a very considerable payment of pigs from his charge's father."[28] Before a girl can marry she must have her two upper incisor teeth knocked out ceremonially and then remain secluded in her father's hut for ten days;[29] but this is an individual, not a group rite.

The *Manuans*. At about the time of the appearance of the secondary sex characteristics a group of boys are circumcised together; this group always consists of an even number of youths (two, four, or six), and those who have been circumcised together enter into a ritualized relationship with each other.[30] There are no *rites de passage* for girls at this time.

The *Murngin.* After being subjected to extrusion and brother-sister avoidance, the young boy is circumcised, and learns the ceremonial secrets of Murngin society.[31] There are no such rites for the girls, and they are subjected only to the rules of brother-sister avoidance.

The *Navaho.* Both boys and girls go through a religious ceremonial at about the time of the appearance of the secondary sex characteristics, but these do not include either seclusion or mutilation. "Boys and girls are made recognized members of The People and are introduced to full participation in ceremonial life by a short initiation ceremony which usually occurs on the next to last night of a Night Way."[32]

The *Papago.* There are no *rites de passage* for either boys or girls, but there is a purification ceremony carried out for an individual girl by her parents at the time of her first menstruation.[33]

The *Pukapukans.* "No surgical operation or physical manipulation was performed on the Pukapukan boy or girl."[34] The end of childhood and the onset of adolescence occurs somewhere around the age of fifteen when boys and girls, who formerly went about naked, were allowed to put on clothes. "If a boy should try to wear a malo or a girl a kilt (*titi*) before the parents consider them mature, the parents would tear the garment off and make the young persons wait. The parents judge maturity by the secondary sex characteristics or by comparison with the other children of the same birth class."[35] Malo and kilt are donned by a group of boys or girls who belong to the same age-grade, and each age-grade goes through its formal initiatory ceremony together and about six months after the preceding group.

The *Tallensi*. There are no ceremonies or rites performed for children of either sex at the appearance of the secondary sex characteristics.[36]

The *Tanala*. There are no ceremonies or rites of any sort for either sex at the appearance of the secondary sex characteristics.[37]

The *Thonga*. Boys go through a very elaborate and lengthy *rite de passage* at about the time of the appearance of the secondary sex characteristics. These ceremonies take place every four or five years, and incorporate seclusion, instruction, and circumcision.[38] No rites or ceremonies are performed for girls at this time.[39]

The *Tikopia*. At the appearance of the secondary sex characteristics, Tikopia boys undergo a *rite de passage*, the climax of which is the circumcision of a group of boys.[40]

The *Trobrianders*. The Trobrianders do not mark the appearance of the secondary sex characteristics in either sex with any rites or ceremonies.

The following are the societies of the sample in which children are brought up for sociological independence:

The *Alorese*. "Neither sex has any ritually or socially recognized crisis rites to dramatize the passage from childhood to adulthood. It is basically an individual and personal transition that must be made."[41]

The *Balinese*. There are no *rites de passage* at the emergence of the secondary sex characteristics,[42] although there are ceremonies for individual upper caste girls when they reach menarche; these personal rites vary from village to village.[43]

The *Camayurá*. With the appearance of the secondary sex characteristics, a boy or a girl is secluded individually behind a screen for a limited period of time, during which they are educated in adult practices and beliefs by their parents.[44]

Cañamelar. There are no *rites de passage* for either sex at the appearance of the secondary sex characteristics.[45]

The *Chamorros*. There are no initiation ceremonies at the appearance of the secondary sex characteristics.[46]

The *Chenchu*. There are no observances of the emergence of the secondary sex characteristics either among boys or girls.[47]

Chimaltenango. "There is no sudden transition from childhood to adult life, and in keeping with this there are no ceremonies demarcating adolescence."[48]

The *Dusan*. No ritual or ceremonial notice is taken of the transition from childhood to adolescence.[49]

The *Copper Eskimo*. There are no rites or ceremonials at the appearance of the secondary sex characteristics.[50]

The *Fijians*. Formerly, the Fijians practiced group circumcision — as well as extrusion — at the appearance of the secdonary sex characteristics. "Today's young men are circumcised separately at ten or twelve. They have no *tubu-tubu* [matrilineal kinsman, grandfather or mother's brother] to nurse their convalescence."[51]

The *Ifaluk*. No ceremonial or ritual recognition is given to the appearance of the secondary sex characteristics in boys. but a girl undergoes an individual ceremony with members of her family and kin group at the time of her menarche.[52]

The *Kaingang*. They do not appear to have any ceremonies or rites for either sex at the appearance of the secondary sex characteristics.[53]

The *Kaska*. "No social recognition marks the transition to puberty in the boy or girl."[54]

The *Kwakiutl*. At about the time of the appearance of the secondary sex characteristics, a boy gives his first *potlatch* — a feast at which a man gives away coppers and blankets and which his matched opponent must repay with one hundred per cent interest. When a girl reaches puberty her father gives a *potlatch* for her, but otherwise there are no ceremonials or rites to mark the transition to adolescence.[55]

The *Lakher*. "There are no ceremonies connected with the attainment of puberty."[56]

The *Lepcha*. "Theoretically they ignore physical puberty, have no word or words to express it, and pay no sort of formal attention to its arrival."[57]

The *Marquesans*. No formal notice was taken of the appearance of a boy's secondary sex characteristics, and a private rite was held for a girl at her first menstruation.[58]

The *Midlanders*. No ritual or ceremonial recognition is taken of the appearance of the secondary sex characteristics in either boys or girls.[59]

Mirebalais. There are no initiation ceremonies for either sex at the appearance of the secondary sex characteristics.[60]

Moche. There do not appear to be any observances for either sex at the appearance of the secondary sex characteristics.[61]

The *Nama* Hottentots. The Nama used to have true initiation ceremonies for boys at the appearance of the secondary sex characteristics, but these have completely disappeared.[62] A private rite is held for a girl by her family at the time of her first menstruation, but there do not appear to be any group ceremonies.[63]

The *Ojibwa*. Formerly, the Ojibwa used to practice brother-sister avoidance. "This began when the boy's voice commenced to change, and when the girl first menstruated."[64] There is a ceremonial fast for boys at the time of the appearance of the secondary sex characteristics, but such fasts had occurred since early childhood; there is also a ceremonial fast for a girl at menarche, but hers is much less important than the boy's. Otherwise, no ceremonial recognition is taken of the transition to adolescence.[65]

Okinawa. There are no *rites de passage* for either boys or girls at the appearance of the secondary sex characteristics.[66]

The *Omaha*. There were no *rites de passage* at the appearance of the secondary sex characteristics for either boys or girls, although boys underwent longer individual fasts than in early childhood.[67]

Rocky Roads. No social recognition is given to the appearance of the secondary sex characteristics in either boys or girls.[68]

The *Sanpoil*. There are no ceremonies or rites for either sex at the appearance of the secondary sex characteristics.[69]

The *Shtetl*. No *rites de passage* were held for girls at menarche.[70] On his thirteenth birthday, a boy went through an individual ritual, called *bar mitzvah*, in which he was admitted to full participation in religious ritual; this was never a group ceremony, and it never involved seclusion or mutilation.[71]

The *Sirionó*. "There are no rites or ceremonies for boys at the appearance of the secondary sex characteristics, but there are group *rites de passage* for girls at around the time of menarche from which men are rigidly excluded."[72]

The *Slave*. There were no *rites de passage* at the appearance of the secondary sex characteristics for either boys or girls.[73]

Suye Mura. The appearance of the secondary sex characteristics is unmarked socially for either boys or girls.[74]

Taitou. No sociological recognition is taken of the appearance of the secondary sex characteristics in either boys or girls, and the transition from childhood to adolescence is "gradual."[75]

The *Tarascans*. There are no rites or ceremonials for either sex at the appearance of the secondary sex characteristics.[76]

The *Teton Dakota*. There are no rites or observances at the time of the appearance of either boys' or girls' secondary sex characteristics.[77]

The *Witoto*. There are no *rites de passage* for either boys or girls at the appearance of the secondary sex characteristics.[78]

The *Yakut*. No ritual or ceremonial recognition is given to the appearance of the secondary sex characteristics in either boys or girls.[79]

The *Yurok*. There is a ten-day seclusion period for girls at menarche but there are no *rites de passage* for girls or boys at this point in the life-cycle.[80]

The *Zadruga*. There were no rites or ceremonies for either boys or girls at the appearance of the secondary sex characteristics, and the transition to adolescence was mild and gradual.[81]

SIX

LIVING WITH A SENSE
OF RESPONSIBILITY

H ow can we know wheth-
er a society arranges its institutions around the value of
sociological interdependence, and that it requires that the
individual be anchored in the wider kin group? Similarly,
how can we know that a society arranges its institutions
around the value of sociological independence, and that
it requires that the individual be anchored in the nuclear
family? The variables of social-emotional anchorage and a
sense of identity are too abstract and qualitative to be observed directly. Hence, an independent criterion of this behavior is needed. I suggest that it can be found in the society's legal system.

Erikson has observed that " 'loyal' and 'legal' have the
same root, linguistically and psychologically."[1] Loyalty surely has many sources, but I am concerned here with only
two of them, namely, the sociological and the psychological.

From a sociological point of view, loyalty must always
be considered as stemming from and residing in highly specific group and boundary-maintaining systems. Thus, when
we look at one individual in a society, his loyalties — to his
friends, to his spouse, to his children, to his kinsmen and

the like — are of entirely different orders and connote different kinds of relationships. A person is never loyal in the abstract, and his loyalties take entirely different forms in different social matrixes.

From a psychological point of view, loyalty is a derivative and a dimension of emotional identification with another person, or with respect to a sociological boundary-maintaining system such as a kin group or a nation. In psychological terms, loyalty can be defined in terms of a sense of responsibility: "The extent to which the individual feels responsible for what other people are doing, gives a clue to his degree of identification with those people."[2] A sense of responsibility, in turn, is institutionalized in the legal system of a society. Thus, if loyalty — the sense of responsibility — is intimately related to emotional identification, then both can be viewed on the same plane of abstraction and it is possible to seek independent evidence for them in a society's legal institutions.

Since mature and healthy adult identification with another person is never complete identification, and since a sense of responsibility is one manifestation of identification and a sense of identity, it follows logically that even though people may feel responsible for the actions of those with whom they identify, they can never be expected to feel completely responsible for all of each other's actions. Furthermore, since anchorage in the boundary-maintaining system of the nuclear family is of a different order than anchorage in a bounded descent group, we should not only expect to find different modes of identification under these different conditions, but we should also expect to find different institutional forms of the sense of responsibility.

[128]

Briefly stated, an individual is not expected to assume responsibility for the actions of other people in societies organized around the value of sociological independence, while he is sometimes expected to assume the onus for the actions of his lineage- or clan-mates in societies that arrange their institutions around the value of sociological interdependence.

There has been an unfortunate tradition in anthropology in which clanship *per se* has been seen as automatically setting certain consequences into motion. We have already noted in connection with the upbringing of children that clanship constitutes a set of preconditions that might or might not be set into motion, depending on the over-all value system of the society. Similar patterns can be observed in the distribution of food in pre-industrialized societies.[3] In the field of law, however, the tradition persists, and following the lead set by Radcliffe-Brown in 1933,[4] Hoebel has written, "Because it is such a potent institution, the clan looms large in the law of horticultural societies. And looming large, it intensifies the problems of maintenance of social order. Clan solidarity commits the clan to challenge, 'Strike my brother and you strike me.' An offense against an individual is an offense against the entire clan. The reaction is collective, and a single disturbance can set hundreds of people into action."[5] This is simply not true.

Every known human society has a system of law. There are many aspects to any legal system; the one that is relevant here as an independent criterion of a sense of responsibility is the concept of legal liability. Despite the difficulties involved in the comparisons of legal systems, there are characteristics that all seem to share. The first is that any body of law is dependent on and exists within the totality of the institutions and experiences of a society. The second — and it is this with which I shall be primarily concerned — is the concept of liability and responsibility. This concept specifies which actions incur penalties when they are committed, and for which actions an individual is legally responsible and must assume liability. The penalties and punishments that inevitably follow from the perpetration of an illegal action are imposed by a human agency — as distinct from a supernatural — and incur a predetermined, commensurate and specifiable loss of life, limb, freedom of movement, privileges, rights, or property.

Not all societies hold people liable for the same acts. For example, premediated murder is not considered criminal in all societies; similarly, even when it is considered criminal, such homicide sets different kinds of liability into motion in different societies. In some, an individual has to answer to the state or some other corporate political body for his act, while in others the state can exact punishment not only from the murderer himself but also from his kinsmen. Among still other peoples, the murdered man's kinsmen can seek out the actual culprit or the latter's kinsmen and, on their own initiative, avenge the death of their fellow group member.

The heart of any legal system is in its concept of liability. As soon as an individual commits an act which, according to the legal system of his society, is in violation of the legal norms of the group, he incurs the theoretical possibility of being punished or forced to make restitution.

Theory and practice usually coincide, for in every society it is expected that an individual will assume responsibility for every act that he commits. But every legal system anticipates the possibility that the gears of theory and practice may fail to mesh. A murderer may escape and cannot be punished; a thief may have consumed or destroyed his loot and cannot make restitution; a malevolent magician cannot be apprehended, but the magical act must be punished if its evil effects are to be dissipated; a woman may commit adultery, and although the law of the society stipulates that she is liable for her behavior and that it is punishable by a fine paid to her husband, the rules also state that a woman is a legal minor and, therefore, cannot be expected to pay a fine; and so forth. What, then, can be done if the legally specified punishment cannot be carried out? Each legal system must deal with this possibility in one way or another; but the way in which the problem is dealt with must be in harmony with the total value system of the society. The legal concept of responsibility must be consonant with the feelings of responsibility that people hold, the legal system of a society being but one part of its total value system.

In some societies, such as our own, if an individual can escape punishment for an illegal act, the punishment cannot be meted out — or, as some would say, "justice is not done." But there are other societies in which punishment can be meted out whether or not it is the actual culprit who is punished or makes the necessary restitution.

These differences imply divergent legal structures, and the diversity between systems of law in this respect is clear and rather simple. On the one hand, there are legal structures based on the principle of "several" or strictly individual liability (from the verb "to sever"). In legal systems

built on this basis, every individual is held liable and responsible for his actions and his actions only; no one else
can be held responsible or liable for another's act. If, in
such societies, a person can escape his liability for an illegal act, punishment is not meted out and the liability is
not met.

In other legal systems, however, we find the principle of
"joint" liability. This means that if — and only if — the per-
petrator of an unlawful act cannot be apprehended or meet
his legal liability, then — and only then — his liability falls
on members of his descent group. Thus, if murder automatically sets liability into motion — a retaliatory murder,
let us say — one of the culprit's kinsmen will have to assume the onus if the actual culprit escapes. If, in such a
society, a man trespasses or steals or damages another's
property and is required by law to make restitution, members of his descent group will have to make payment if the
culprit is unable to do so. If this type of legal system stipulates that a woman's adultery must be compensated for
in money, but if she cannot be held personally liable for
her behavior, specified members of her descent group must
make the payments to her husband.

This is quite different from the view of clan-law held by
many anthropologists and exemplified in the statement by
Hoebel quoted above. Life in most societies is too orderly
and social life is too deeply based on self-control for any
social system to allow "a single disturbance [to] set hundreds of people into action"[6] in any uncontrolled way,
other than in altogether exceptional circumstances. Even in
warfare rigid control is usually maintained by leaders over
the "collective reaction" of defenders of the society; war-

fare itself threatens the boundary-maintaining system of the society. An individual's illegal act, such as murder, theft, arson, trespass, or adultery, does not threaten the boundaries of the total society; hence, it cannot and does not set masses of people into action except under the most extraordinary circumstances.

When a man commits murder in a society whose legal system contains the principle of joint liability, the consequences largely depend on the circumstances of the action; accident, self-defense, provocation, and so forth, may provide extenuation. The identity of the murderer in relation to his victim is also important in this connection. If one clansman has killed another, and if it is clear that the homicide was premeditated, the culprit will be executed or banished or punished in some other way. Rarely if ever does the rule of joint liability obtain when a murder has taken place within the clan or lineage, even when the culprit has managed to escape punishment — except in some civil states, such as Dahomey — for in such a case the clan would, in effect, be turning on itself. One of the functions of clan-vengeance in a case of homicide is to maintain a balance of strength between groups that are often competitive. This goal would not be served in applying the rule of joint liability within the kin group. This produces the interesting parenthetical observation that joint liability is in part a principle governing relationships between groups. My principal concern here, however, is with the values governing relationships within groups.

When a society's legal system contains joint liability, it is invoked when a man of one clan has killed a member of a different clan or other kin group. But the procedure is extremely orderly and is controlled by explicit rules. These almost always specify which kinsmen of the victim have the responsibility of avenging the death; it is never the entire clan or lineage that is set into avenging motion. The rules also state that the avengers can apply the rule of joint liability only if the killer cannot be apprehended, and that the vengeance must be confined to specified kinsmen of the actual culprit; they cannot kill just any member of the killer's kin group.

As I have observed elsewhere (in connection with the distribution of food in preliterate societies), the primary and significant communications of social life take place along and are made possible by the existing institutional lines of the society. Thus, no society allows for the random and promiscuous expression of feelings. Rather, feelings may be communicated, whether verbally, physically, or materially, only to certain people. These lines of communication are almost everywhere specified, structuralized, and consistent; they are, in essence, institutionalized.[6a]

Among the many purposes which the institutionalization of lines of communication serves is that it helps people to meet the need for predictability in social relationships. A sense of anchorage and a socio-emotional identity are communications to others as well as to oneself about one's feelings about oneself and others within a social boundary-system. These communications culminate in the sense of responsibility appropriate to the institutional arrangements of the society, which the individual also takes as his own. Like all other meaningful communications, the expression of the sense of responsibility must be highly predictable, especially in view of its involvement with one's socio-emotional identity.

Such predictability, and its attendant personal stability, would be precluded if an entire clan were permitted to seek out *any* member of another clan to avenge a homicide.

Pospisil cites the following illustrative case from among the Kapauku of Papuan New Guinea:[7]

> *Place*: Kego (South Kamu)
> *Date*: ca. 1948
> *Parties*:
> a) *Defendant*: Ed Tun of Dege
> b) *Murdered Man*: Iw Gek of Kego.
> c) *Authority*: Ed Pai of Dege.
> d) *Executioner*: younger brother of the killed man.
> e) *Man executed*: Ed Tod of Dege (FaBrSo of the murderer).
>
> *Facts*: Someone had destroyed the traps of Gek. He charged the defendent with the crime and a stick fight resulted. A few days later the defendant murdered Gek by shooting him from ambush.
>
> *Outcome*: Although the murdered man belonged to a different political unit, the authority, in order to prevent war, extradited the defendant to the Iw people for punishment. Since the culprit escaped into the jungle and could not be found for approximately ten months, the brother of the murdered man lost his patience and killed the FaBrSo of the refugee. Thus, the dead on both sides were matched and peace restored.

The "vendetta" is one form of joint liability, and it must be distinguished from the "feud". A feud is a chronic state of hostilities between two groups in which, usually, they simply hate each other. A vendetta is often called "blood vengeance" or "blood feud." In its most literal meaning it is the rule that the nearest relative of a murdered person — usually his son or brother — is obligated to take revenge on the murderer or, if he should escape, on the murderer's nearest relative. When people hold to the rule of vendetta, reprisal is usually accepted by the community of the original culprit and the original killing is considered to be expiated. This rule can function smoothly only when both groups subscribe to it. If the group on which revenge has been taken does not agree, a pitched war is likely to result. But in most cases, at least in this respect, contiguous groups tend to hold similar values and attitudes.

While the vendetta is a form of joint liability, not all joint liability involves vendetta. The latter refers to the vengeance which is inflicted by the members of one group upon a person of another group. But there are other forms of joint liability, such as that which is sometimes invoked by the king or some other civil state agency in societies organized into clans.

Even when a legal system has within it the principle of joint liability, this tenet rarely obtains in connection with more than three or four types of actionable behavior; otherwise, the prevailing principle is that of several (individual) liability. Therefore, the relevant cross-cultural generalization here is that all societies have the principle of several liability in their legal systems, but some have the principle of joint liability as well.

This parallels the principle that in all societies children identify with their parents, but in some societies children also identify with other members of their kin groups. A further parallel exists in that just as mature and healthy identification is never complete, so joint liability never applies to all unlawful acts committed by a kinsman in those societies in which it obtains.

My criterion for anchorage in the wider kin group — sociological interdependence — is the existence of the principle of joint liability in a society's legal system, and my criterion for anchorage in the nuclear family — sociological independence — is the presence only of several liability in the society's legal system.

A sense of identity implies social values that people have about themselves in relation to each other within the groups in which they are anchored. That is, a sense of identity implies one or another form of the sense of responsibility which is codified in their legal structures. With anchorage in the family or in the wider kin group, therefore, and with different values associated with these different anchorages, specific psychological processes must occur within the people who live by these principles.

It would be a serious mistake, however, to equate joint liability with sociological interdependence, or to assert that several liability and sociological independence are one and the same. I assume simply that the concept of liability obtaining in a society's legal system — whether joint or several — is a manifestiation of the society's pivotal values of interdependence or independence, of how human relationships should be ordered. I further assume that these concepts of liability can be used as independent criteria of interdependence and independence. Both theorems are necessary to understand how the individual "self" stands *vis-à-vis* principles of legal liability and responsibility, especially in view of the postulate that the legal concepts of responsibility must be in harmony with the feelings of responsibility obtaining in a society.

It is my contention that the emotional patterns underlying a system of joint liability must emerge out of cataclysmic experiences during periods of momentous vulnerability and psychological exposure. These periods, I have hypothesized, occur during the transition from childhood to adolescence, and especially during the first stage of puberty. At the same time, however, the practices of extrusion, brother-sister avoidance, and initiation ceremonies, together with their concomitant patterns of socialization by members of the child's descent group, are responses of the parental generation to the particular kind of social and value system in and for which they are bringing up their children.[8] Clan or lineage organization appears to be the most conducive to this particular pattern of socialization and its institutional manifestations, but it does not guarantee that these will occur; nor is it indispensable to maturing and developing in this fashion.

If an individual is brought up for many years to experience his anchorage within the wider kin group, if his identifications are with the members of his descent group, if his sense of identity — and, therefore, his sense of responsibility — are tied to his descent group, we observe the preconditions for the social value of sociological interdependence around which the society's institutions can be organized.

But how can a person maintain self-awareness if he assumes responsibility for the actions of others and if others assume responsibility for his actions? How, in other words, can a person maintain an identity if he is unable to equate himself with his own actions and he cannot say, "I have done this," and thus be aware that his "self" coincides with his actions? Social chaos would result, and confusion would be a consequence in every person in the group. If an individual did not have to assume responsibility for his own actions, he would not feel impelled to get anything done and he would expect everyone else to take care of him. Can there be no individual responsibility in a society with the principle of joint liability?

The two concepts of legal liability thus appear to conflict, for they cannot be applied simultaneously. The general restriction of joint liability to no more than two or three kinds of actions seems to be paradoxical: would it not be more consistent to apply one or the other principle throughout the legal system? This would be the case if principles of liability were manifestations only of the kinship organization, as in the view of Radcliffe-Brown exemplified in the formulation by Hoebel quoted earlier.

An alternative — the one I am suggesting here — is to view the concept of legal liability as a manifestation of social values and feelings of responsibility. In this light, and because of the need to maintain individual self-awareness, the restriction of joint liability to no more than two or three actions is a "token" or "symbolic" representation of the value of sociological interdependence. This symbolism connotes an extreme degree of cohesiveness within a boundary-maintaining kin group and involving the deepest emotional bonds with kinsmen. It is a manifestation of the consciousness of social-emotional anchorage and a sense of identity. The retention and application of the principle of individual liability for all other actions is an institutional means of satisfying the requirement of the individual's maintenance of self-awareness through responsibility for his own actions.*

In summary: I have tried to show that the process of growing up and acquiring a particular sense of identity and anchorage results from the confluence of two forces within the individual: his biology — or his biologically-rooted crises — and the goals and values the society has impressed on him through its institutions. I have also tried to show how the child is manipulated physically and emotionally with respect to the boundaries of his family in order to inculcate in him one or another sense of social identity and anchorage. I have further maintained that whether the child's relationship to his family is interfered with by moving him out of its boundaries, or whether he is left within its boundaries, depends on the goals and values of the society. But these goals begin to be realized within the society even before the first stage of puberty. Thus, if youngsters are to be brought up for sociological interdependence, they will be taught by members of their descent groups in addition to their parents, so that they will develop emotional identifications within the boundaries of that wider group. If children are to be brought up for sociological independence, they will be taught by their parents plus people who are not members of any boundary-maintaining groups within which such identifications can take place.

In order to secure evidence for the existence of these al-

---

*American corporation law is not a form of joint liability. This legal concept applies only within primary groups, while a modern corporation is a secondary group; investor-members are not liable for the acts of the corporate officials.

ternative value systems, I have examined a number of legal systems and their formal statements of liability and responsibility; this examination leads to the following, concluding hypotheses:

(1) *In those societies in which children are brought up by their parents as well as by members of the children's descent group, and in which children are subjected to extrusion or brother-sister avoidance at the first stage of puberty, the concept of joint liability will be found.*

(2) *In those societies in which children are brought up by their parents plus non-members of the children's descent group, and in which there is neither extrusion nor brother-sister avoidance, only the concept of several liability will be found.*

The data for these hypotheses are summarized in Table 7; Table 8 summarizes the data for all the cross-cultural hypotheses tested thus far.

Table 7

Relationships between Experiences in Growing Up
and Concept of Legal Liability

	Joint Liability	Several Liability
Socialization by parents plus members of child's descent group, etc.	27	1
Socialization by parents plus non-members of child's descent group, etc.	1	36
$X^2 = 53.32$	$T = .91$	$p < .001$

Table 8

Relationship of the Principle of Descent to Modes of
Socialization and Legal Principles

	Unilinear	Bilateral
Socialization by parents plus members of the child's descent group AND		
Extrusion and/or avoidance, initiation, and joint liability	16	1e
Extrusion and/or avoidance, and joint liability	8	2f
Initiation only and joint liability	0	0
Extrusion, initiation, and several liability	1a	0
Socialization by parents plus non-members of child's descent group AND		
Neither extrusion nor avoidance nor initiation, but several liability	16	18
Extrusion and several liability	1b	0
Initiation and several liability	1c	0
Neither extrusion nor avoidance nor initiation, but joint liability	1d	0

a	Lesu	c	Sirionó	e	Manua
b	Lakher	d	Omaha	f	Andamanese and Chiricahua Apache

Living with a Sense of Responsibility

Of the twenty-eight societies described below in which children are brought up by their parents plus members of of their descent group, and in which there is extrusion or brother-sister avoidance, twenty-seven have the concept of joint legal liability in their legal systems. Only one society (the Lesu) appear to constitute an exception to the hypothesis, and I am unable to offer an explanation for this divergent case.

The *Andaman Islanders*, who practice extrusion by sending children to friends or relatives, define as anti-social such actions as murder, wounding another person, theft, damage to another's property, and adultery. The concept of joint liability obtains among the Andamanese, and it applies only in the area of murder. A murderer usually tries to escape into the jungle to avoid the vengeance of the deceased's relatives, and they try to find him there. If they fail they usually attempt to take the life of one of his kinsmen.[9]

The *Chiricahua Apache*, who usually build separate dwellings for young boys, apply the principle of joint liability to murder and theft. In the case of murder, the murdered man's relatives are obligated to avenge his death, and if they cannot punish the murderer, the latter's relatives will either have to make payment to the deceased's group or one of them may be killed instead; if a man is a thief and cannot make restitution, one of his relatives will attempt to make the payment for him.[10]

The *Arapesh*, who extrude girls and initiate boys, state that if a man kills another and cannot be apprehended, one of his clansmen can be killed in his stead.[11]

The *Arunta*, who practice a limited form of brother-sister avoidance and a series of initiation rites for boys, state that

if a man kills another, the latter's kinsmen are under obliga-
tion to avenge the death, either by taking the life of the
murderer or of one of his kinsmen. Spencer and Gillen, de-
scribing in detail the events of an expedition to avenge the
murder of a band-member, wrote: "It transpired that upon
this particular occasion the avenging party had not killed
the man whom they actually went in search of. He had some-
how got news of their coming, and had discreetly cleared
away to a distant part of the country. As they could not kill
him they had speared his father, under the plea that the old
man had known all about his son going . . . to kill the Alice
Springs man, and had not attempted to prevent him from
doing so."[12]

The *Bantu* of North Kavirondo, Logoli and Vugusu, who
extrude boys and girls and initiate boys, hold clan members
responsibile for the actions of others in cases of child negli-
gence or a woman's adultery. If a woman commits adultery,
either her father or the latter's kinsmen must pay compensation to her husband.[13] "If the injuries [to a child], e.g. burns,
are attributed to the carelessness of the mother, the father of
the child can claim damages from his wife's father or brothers (as those responsible for her conduct), if to the carelessness of the father, the child's mother's relatives can claim
damages from the father of the child or his kinsmen."[14]

The *Basuto*, who extruded boys and initiated boys and
and girls, have been in the process of undergoing a complete
change in their culture and social structure; traditionally,
prior to European contact, they had the concept of joint
liability in their customary legal system.[15] Today, their
"legislative and judicial institutions have now given place
almost entirely to those of European origin."[16]

The *Bena*, who extruded boys and girls and initiated girls only in their traditional culture, possessed the concept of joint liability as part of their legal system. "Murder... could formerly be punished by private vengeance. In fact, the dead man's relatives were theoretically in honor bound to avenge his death by the death of the murderer or one of his relatives."[17]

The *Bushmen*, who practice extrusion for both sexes, confine the principle of joint liability to murder, and it is stated as follows: "If the slayer himself is dead or out of reach, the feud extends to his nearest male relative."[18]

The *Chagga*, whose boys are extruded and initiated, hold that a man's kinsmen can be held liable and responsible if he commits a murder or a theft and if restitution cannot be extracted from him personally.[19]

The *Dahomeans*, who extrude both sexes but initiate boys only, maintain that the individual is not treated as an isolated unit. If he was involved in a dispute, his family was also involved. Thus, "when a man was accused of a crime, that is, of a breach of civil law, his effects were forfeited to the King, his domestic relations and friends were seized, some were executed, others were sold as slaves."[20]

The *Gros Ventres*, who extruded girls, generally felt that if time could be allowed to elapse between a murder and the revenge, passions would cool, but, ideally, a murderer's kins- men "collectively shared responsibility for the crime."[21]

The *Hopi*, who extrude boys and initiate both sexes, do not appear to apply the concept of joint liability to murder or theft, but "clans, as such, may be blamed for the cere- monial misdeeds of their members."[22]

The *Jukun*, who extruded and initiated boys, held to the

principle of joint liability, and confined it to the revenge of murder and witchcraft. "In olden days when murders were rife it was the maternal uncle rather than the father who took vengeance for the loss of a member of his kin. The father would report the matter to the maternal uncle, who would, if a strong man, take life for life, without even obtaining the sanction of the chief. And if the maternal uncle could not kill the actual murderer he would endeavor to kill, not the son of the murderer, but the sister's son. Furthermore . . . if a person was convicted of witchcraft and was, with his relatives, put to death or sold into slavery, the relatives involved were relatives in the female and not the male line."[23]

The *Kurtatchi*, who extrude both sexes and initiate only the boys, hold to the principle of joint liability in cases of theft, as an ideal principle, which may or may not be put into practice depending on the preference of the victim.[24]

The *Kwoma*, who extrude the boys and initiate both sexes, also confine the application of the concept of joint liability to theft, for which a man's uncle may be held liable.[25]

The *Lamba*, who extrude boys and girls to age-villages, have a formalized system of judicial courts in which the principle of joint liability can be applied as part of a judgment in a case of murder. If a chief, sitting as judge, desires, "he sends men to arrest the sisters and mother of the accused. When they are brought, some of the women are handed over to the relatives of the deceased as slaves, others are retained by the chief."[26]

The *Lesu* who extrude and initiate the boys, appear to constitute an exception to my hypothesis, and the concept or principle of joint responsibility does not obtain in connection with any legal actions.[27]

The *Malekula,* who practice extrusion and initiation for boys, hold to the principle of joint liability in connection with murder. Every murder has to be avenged, whether or not the person on whom vengeance has been taken was responsible for the act.[28]

The *Manuans,* who practice brother-sister avoidance and male initiation rites, apply the principle of joint liability to three kinds of anti-social behavior, specifically, murder, insult, or adultery. In all such actions, it is not only the individual who is liable and responsible but his relatives and the head of his relationship grouping as well.[29]

The *Murngin,* who practice brother-sister avoidance, extrusion for boys, and male initiation rites, hold that every wound and every murder must be avenged either by wounding or killing the actual culprit or, if he cannot be apprehended, a member of his kin group.[30]

The *Navaho,* who extrude the boys, in their traditional culture, appear to have applied the principle of joint liability to no less than five classes of anti-social behavior: murder, theft, rape, debts, and witchcraft. "All clansmen were responsible for the crimes and debts of other members of their clan, hence it was in their own interest to prevent murder, rape, and theft on the part of any and all clan relatives."[31] In contemporary Navaho society, witchcraft has increased and is difficult to control, but "in the old days . . . if a member of clan A in a given local group accused a member of clan B of witchcraft or if there was any evidence which the Navaho would consider as indication of the practice of witchcraft against a member of clan B, the whole of Clan A would have to contribute to a fine. Such practices meant severe punishments to the culprit from his clan relatives whom he normally counted on for his major emotional support."[32]

The *Papago*, who extrude both sexes, state the rule that "ceremonial payments falling upon one member were made by the whole group or by that member who could best afford it. Vengeance for murder — a rare occurrence — fell on any member of the group who was available."[33]

The *Pukapuka*, who extruded boys and girls, applied the principle of joint liability to willful murder and to theft. In the case of murder, the maternal sub-lineage of the culprit had the choice, apparently, either of punishing the murderer or of assuming "collective responsibility for the crime."[34]

The *Tallensi*, who extrude the boys, hold to the principle of joint legal liability only in the matter of the payment of debts. "Thus in the old days a creditor could raid the livestock of any clansman of his debtor, but not those of a neighbor of his debtor who belonged to a different clan. In the latter case a reprisal raid was the penalty."[35] Where a clansman was raided for the debt of his kin, the former could demand restitution from the man who had incurred the original debt, but he had no claim against the creditor who carried out the raid.

The *Tanala*, who practiced extrusion for boys, applied the principle of joint liability within a very narrow range. "The maintenance of order was in the hands of the [chiefs] . . . . Each [village chief] was personally responsible to the king for the behavior of his followers and might, in extreme cases, be fined.[36]

The *Thonga*, who extrude both sexes and initiate the boys, restrict the application of the principle of joint liability to matters of debt; they "consider relatives as responsible for the debts of their own kin."[37]

[148]

The *Tikopia*, who extrude children to homes of distant kinsmen and initiate the boys, also restrict the application of the principle of joint liability to one area of behavior, namely the responsibility of a group of kinsmen for a man who abducts a woman to be his wife; in their liability, these kinsmen must make restitutive payments to the woman's kin group.[38]

The *Trobrianders*, who practice brother-sister avoidance and male extrusion, confine the concept of joint liability to cases of murder, in which the kinsmen of the culprit have to pay blood-money to the relatives of the victim.[39]

Now let us turn to those societies in which the hypothesized preconditions for joint liability do not obtain in order to learn whether, as predicted, they possess only the concept of several (individual) legal liability.

The patrilineal *Alorese*, when a murder is committed, tend to start a series of feuds in which one killing provokes another. The principle obtaining in their legal system appears to be one of several liability, since a retaliatory murder against a relative of an escaped culprit is seen as another provocative act and not a just compensation for the original murder committed.[40]

The bilateral *Balinese* have their lives organized "on a principle of voluntary associations with others as a member of a village, a rice club, a temple club, an orchestra, etc., and membership carries with it obligations and privileges; failure to discharge or claim these is punished by fines and finally by expulsion."[41] This is the limit of jointly assumed responsibility, and legal liability among the Balinese is several.[42]

The *Camayurá* legal system is predicated entirely on the principle of several liability. Their kinship is bilateral. "Besides banishment from the tribe there appears to be no other way of punishing injuries committed by one person against another."[43]

Cañamelar is subject to the Western legal system which governs all of Puerto Rico and there do not seem to be any local customary departures from the principle of several liability.[44]

The *Chamorros* were formerly matrilineal; currently, they are bilateral and are governed by the American legal system which is administered by the civil government of Guam and in which the principle of individual liability and responsibility obtains entirely.[45]

The *Chenchu* legal system holds each individual responsible only for his own actions; their kinship system is bilateral. "The support lent by clansmen in a dispute, is at the best moral, and falls definitely short of any close identification. There is no collective action and no collective responsibility in the clan.[46]

Chimaltenango, which is patrilineal, seems to live entirely by the code of law which governs all of Guatemala and there appears to be only several legal liability.[47]

The bilateral *Dusun* have an elaborate legal system in which each penalty and each extenuating circumstance is worked out for all actions which are deemed anti-social, and in all there is only individual liability and responsibility.[48]

The bilateral *Copper Eskimo* have few, if any, mechanisms for the enforcement of justice, and vengeance is rarely exacted for murder even by close kin of the deceased. "For minor offenses ... such as theft and abduction, there is no remedy unless the victim takes the matter into his own hands and exacts compensation or vengeance..... Feuds may be settled occasionally by single combat.[49]

The matrilineal *Fijians* maintain a principle of strict individual liability and responsibility for all offenses.[50]

Ifaluk is matrilineal and is still largely governed by its own native system of laws, in which only several liability appears to obtain.[51]

The patrilineal *Kaingang* live in a social system which is riddled by feuds that are on the verge of destroying their society. In their legal system, however, individual responsibility is "representative of their ideals."[52]

The matrilineal *Kaska* Indians are subject to Canadian law, for which they do not seem to have too much regard; but even in their own system of customary law, strict individual liability is the guiding principle in the application of penalties for anti-social behavior.[53]

The *Kwaikutl*, who live in patrilineal clans, have organized almost their entire social system around the individual quest for honor, wealth, and prestige; similar individualism marks their legal system. Liability and responsibility is individual in nature, but occasionally a murder will provoke a retaliatory murder against someone who is in no way related to the original culprit. Sometimes, a Kwakuitl will be "shamed" by the murder of a member of his family and he will kill another man — unrelated to the first slayer — so that another family will be made to feel the shame of such grief.[54]

The *Lakher*, who also live in patrilineal clans, have a legal system that directs that each individual is solely responsible and liable for his own actions and that no one else assumes another man's responsibilities or liabilities in anv area of action.[55]

The patrilineal *Lepcha* have a system of customary law which is based on the principle that liability and responsibility are purely individual affairs.[56] Within their religious system, however, they believe that if a man commits perjury he and his descendants will die from supernatural causes.[57]

The bilateral and polyandrous *Marquesans* had a well developed legal system in which many different types of offenses were recognized, but in every case liability and responsibility were entirely individual.[58]

The bilateral *Midlanders* of North America live under a legal system which derives from the common law of England and in which all responsibility and liability are individualized in tort and crime.

Mirebalais culture (in Haiti) holds every individual responsible for his own actions; often, even a person's family will not help him if he has flouted family authority and run afoul of the law.[59]

Moche is bilateral and is governed by the national laws of Peru, in which the principle of several liability obtains throughout the legal system.[60]

The patrilineal and patrilocal *Nama* Hottentots possessed the principle of joint liability in their legal system until the end of the nineteenth century, but this concept no longer obtains in their law.[61]

The patrilineal *Ojibwa*, too, once included the principle of joint liability in their legal system, but this appears to have been lost from their culture entirely.[62]

[152]

The patrilineal *Okinawans* have their own system of native courts and customary law in which only the principle of several liability is applied.[63]

The patrilineal *Omaha* appear to constitute an exception to the hypothesis, and the concept of joint liability does obtain in their legal system. They did not practice extrusion, brother-sister avoidance, or initiation. However, "murder might be punished by taking the life of the murderer, or that of one of his clansmen."[64]

Rocky Roads is governed by English common law, as is all of Jamaica, and only the principle of several liability obtains in the formal legal system as well as in the community's system of customary law.[65]

The bilateral *Sanpoil* hold to the principle of individual responsibility only; murder was punished by monetary restitution, and although a murderer's relatives usually helped him in making his payments, they did not pay in his stead.[66]

The bilateral *Shtetl* takes the Old Testament as its legal base-line, and in the adjudication of disputes within the community, only several liability and responsibility obtain.[67]

The matrilineal *Sirionó* have a relatively unelaborated legal system in which only several liability obtains; "everyone is expected to stand up for his own rights and to fulfill his own obligations."[68]

The bilateral *Slave* consider each man to be liable for his own actions, and there do not seem to be any provisions for the assumption of liability by anyone but a guilty party.[69]

Suye Mura, in which kinship is reckoned patrilineally, tends largely to govern its own community affairs without assistance from official Japanese functionaries, and all legal and quasi-legal affairs seem based on the principle of individual liability and responsibility.[70]

Taitou, which is also patrilineal, likewise attempts to deal with all anti-social acts within its own system of social control as much as possible. Although the national Chinese government attempted to apply the principles of joint liability to criminal actions, this local village adjudged each person liable only for his own actions and not for anyone else's; generally, only strangers tend to be turned over to national legal authorities.[71]

The bilateral *Tarascans* of Mexico are governed by a national as well as a customary system which is founded on the principle of several liability only.[72]

The bilateral *Teton-Dakota* today are governed almost exclusively by American federal and state laws, both of which recognize the principle of individual responsibility and liability only.[73]

The patrilineal *Witoto* of the Brazilian Amazon consider the righting of wrongs purely an individual matter and each individual is held liable for his own actions; joint liability is entirely absent.[74]

The patrilineal *Yakut* of Siberia are governed by the principle that each man is liable and responsible for every one of his actions and that no one else assumes such liability or responsibility for him.[75]

The *Yurok* Indians are generally patrilineal, and have an elaborate legal system in which every anti-social action is matched by precise penalties; every action must be accounted for by the individual who has committed it, and there appear to be no provisions for the assumption of joint liability.[76]

The *Zadruga* of Croatia are bilateral and have their own system of customary law in which only several liability obtains.[77]

Thus, of the thirty-seven societies in which children are brought up by their parents plus non-members of their descent group, and in which there is neither extrusion, brother-sister avoidance, nor initiation ceremonies at the second stage of puberty, thirty-six have the concept or principle of several or individual liability only in their legal systems. Only one society (the aboriginal Omaha) appears to constitute an exception to the hypothesis, and I am unable to offer any explanation for this divergence.

PART II

SEVEN

BASES OF THE INCEST TABOO:
THE NEED FOR PRIVACY

S INCE the first stage of puberty consists of physiological changes that presage the child's sexuality as well as other potentialities, and because a basic sociological fact of sexual life is the incest taboo, the climax of inculcating the incest taboo in the child, as noted in the conclusion to chapter 3, has to take place early in the first stage of puberty. The rules of incest, however, are not only proscriptions; they are also implicit socio-cultural guides that govern the directions in which the individual can or should move in seeking sexual liaison.

Several difficulties have confronted inquiries into the universality of the incest taboo. The first has been the confusion of the *core* incest taboos — those forbidding sexual relationships among certain members of the nuclear family — and the *extensive* incest taboos — those prohibiting sexual contact among real or fictive kinsmen beyond the boundaries of the nuclear family. These two types of taboos are distinct from each other, although they do have common characteristics.*

*Aberle *et al.* (1963) do not recognize this difference, and their analysis of "The Incest Taboo and the Mating Patterns of Animals" does not go beyond the previously held position that these taboos minimize sexual competition (Murdock 1949, 260-83) and the deleterious effects of genetic inbreeding. Furthermore, the fact that several people are attracted to the same sexual object does not necessarily mean that they are in competition for that person.

A second difficulty has been the tendency to deal with the core incest taboos — mother-son, father-daughter, brother-sister — as one taboo. Actually, however, the core taboos are composed of three separate prohibitions, and although each is a response to a problem shared with the other two, each is also a response to a unique problem.

A third difficulty has been the tendency, especially in anthropology, to view incest taboos as properties of kinship relationships, and, in turn (though perhaps less often) to see these ties as special cases of the more general category of interpersonal relationships. Although there is merit in classifying incest taboos descriptively within the realm of kinship ties, such an approach still leaves us without an independent variable on which the core and extensive taboos are dependent. That is, since incest rules are kinship rules, it is tautological to try to explain incest taboos by kinship relationships. Kinship can tell us where incest taboos are localized and thus provide the basis for a taxonomy; but kinship cannot explain why incest taboos arise in the first place.

Most social scientists hold the view that there is no biological basis for the incest taboo. In so arguing, and in support of their position, they usually point to the extensions of the incest taboo beyond the nuclear family. For example, they contend that if there is, indeed, a biological basis for the prohibition, how can we explain the fact that a man's cross-cousin is tabooed in one society, a permissible sexual partner in a second, and a required marriage partner in a third? Thus, Beals and Hoijer state: "It is clear, then, that while all human societies define incest and prohibit it, neither the definition nor the prohibitions are precisely alike in every culture. It is this fact which negates the hypothesis that the concept of incest has its roots in biological considerations."[1]

I believe that it is an error to combine the core incest taboos of the nuclear family with the extensions of incest taboos to people outside the nuclear family. The definitions and the prohibitions of incest are in fact precisely alike for the nuclear family in every society however much they may differ outside the family.[2]

To explain why all societies complete the inculcation of the incest taboos at the first stage of puberty and why different societies do this differently, I shall begin by suggesting that these taboos have their ultimate roots in man's biology. There is a factor in man's genetic structure which, in its convergence with social-structural factors, has led to the universal adoption of incest taboos. The constitution of man — biologically and culturally — has compelled him to adopt certain kinds of sexual avoidances.*

The significant factor in man's biological makeup that disposes him to establish incest taboos, at least at the core of the nuclear family, is an innate need for a minimal degree of privacy. By this I mean a need for freedom from extreme emotional and physical stimulation, especially from other people. This need, like all others, increases and decreases in strength as it is unfulfilled, and as it is satisfied; its strength and its position in the personality structure varies among individuals.

*Coult has recently examined a different aspect of this problem and observes that "incest taboos are not merely two sides of the same coin, for they could not then vary independently of one another, as they sometimes do" (Coult 1963a, 267).

In a discussion of the relevance of ethological concepts to the study of human behavior, Kaufman has observed:[3]

It is to be noted that in a number of the most important life situations of animals, namely, social situations, one of the significant behavioral tendencies is to *flee*. In our work with humans [psychoanalysts] have long been aware of the importance of aggressive and sexual tendencies, but it seems we may have overlooked or misinterpreted the importance of fleeing tendencies. For the most part flight has not been given the same motivational status as aggression and sexuality. It has not been understood as being the same kind of basic tendency. Rather it has been conceptualized as a second-order reaction, as a defense. Sexuality and aggression have been thought of as the basic tendencies present within the organism in some mysterious way, in other words, as givens — a kind of vitalistic concept — whereas flight has been considered to be something that occurs only in response to certain stimuli. Well, we now have evidence from animal studies that the action patterns of all three tendencies are built into the organism, and that all three tendencies arise in response to specific causation, both internal and external. It seems likely that the same is true of the human. In fact, observations on the human infant and child, while not yet so well documented from this point of view, do supply evidence of the early presence of action patterns subserving sexuality, aggression, and flight (aversion), and their activation by specific causal factors, internal and external. . . . I suggest that our understanding of human behavior might be enhanced by considering the possibility that the tendency to flee is as basic a tendency as the tendencies to attack and to behave sexually.

Kaufman and I are using different terminology in referring to the same phenomenon. Kaufman is a physician and a psychoanalyst, and his formulation of a need for "flight" is in terms of an activity of the individual organism; as an anthropologist, my formulation of this need as one for "privacy" is in terms of social relationships.

There are several independent sources of evidence for the "need for privacy" to be found in animal ecology and zoology, experimental and developmental psychology, and cultural anthropology. The findings of animal ecologists and zoologists bearing on this innate need result from observations of inborn responses to overcrowing as it affects reproduction, infection, and hypertension. In recent years, data have been synthesized from observations of sub-arctic voles, captive animals in zoos, rats, mice, woodchucks, dogs, guinea pigs, monkeys, lynxes, foxes, and the like.

Among the conclusions reached thus far on the effects of overcrowding in these different species is that crowding *per se* has specific effects on glandular activity, especially in the adrenal and pituitary systems, with the consequences of reduced reproductive rates, lower body resistance to infection, and increased rate and frequency of myocardial infarction. Lemmings thus far appear to constitute an exception to these generalizations. But the lemming is not immune to overcrowding; "for a normally shy and timid creature [he] changes into a bold and at times almost pugnacious animal."[4] These inborn responses to overcrowding appear to be confined to higher animals, and this specificity in the evolutionary scale lends great weight to the postulate that mammals need a considerable amount of "breathing space" and physical-emotional *lebensraum* in order to function adequately. These phenomena have their roots in biology [5]

[163]

Such findings, of course, are not entirely new. "Since 1854 it has been known from experimental evidence that crowded animals may not grow at all and when they do grow do so less rapidly than their uncrowded relatives. Under many conditions crowded animals not only do not grow but they die more readily and frequently reproduce less rapidly than when living in uncrowded populations."[6] The fact that has become much clearer, in the view of Christian,[7] is that the effects of overcrowding are social-psychological, but rooted in biology.

Further weight is given to the postulate of the need for privacy through a juxtaposition of ecological data with those from experimental and developmental psychology. Experimenting with caged rats, Calhoun created complex conditions with different levels of population density, ranging from extreme overcrowding to normal conditions. Under the most crowded conditions, "the consequences of the behavioral pathology we observed were most apparent in the females. Many were unable to carry pregnancy to full term or to survive delivery of their litters if they did. An even greater number, after successfully giving birth, fell short in their maternal functions. Among the males the behavior disturbances ranged from sexual deviation to cannibalism and from frenetic overactivity to a pathological withdrawal from which individuals would emerge to eat, drink and move about only when other members were asleep. The social organization of the animals showed equal disruption . . . . Infant mortality ran as high as 96 per cent among the most disoriented groups in the population."[8] On the other hand, "where population density was lowest, the mortality rate among infants and females was also low. Of the various social environments that developed during the course of the experiments, the brood pens, as we called them, appeared to be the only healthy ones, at least in terms of the survival of the group. The harem females generally made good mothers. They nursed their young, built nests for them and protected them from harm. If any situation arose that a mother considered a danger to her pups, she would pick the infants up one at a time and carry them in her mouth to a safer place. Nothing would distract her from this task until the entire litter had been moved. Half the infants born in the brood pens survived."[9]

The antithesis of overcrowding is not the absence of stimulation; instead, the individual requires an optimal degree of privacy, neither too much nor too little. Writing in 1938, Allee observed that "laboratory work of the last few decades still shows that overcrowding is harmful, but it has also uncovered a no less real, though somewhat slighter, set of ill effects of undercrowding."[10] That people, too, need a minimal degree of stimulation from birth onward is made clear by studies of hospitalism or marasmus,[11] the effects of sensory deprivation,[12] maternal deprivation in monkeys,[13] and social isolation and black magic.[14]

Turning to the evidence for the need for privacy from developmental psychology, observations of infants and young children reveal that each — according to his own rhythm, which also seems to be congenital — periodically needs to diminish or halt stimulation ensuing from the people around him. Just as a growing child, not unlike an adult, needs to be with people for the satisfaction of his needs, so does he also have a periodic need to be without people. Bergman and Escalona noted that children who could be characterized as "sensitive" to an extreme are not only easily stimulated to enjoyment but are also easily hurt;[15] the two traits are related. If a child is forced to remain in contact with people beyond his endurance for stimulation, he will become upset. Adults, too, have such needs for stimulus-reduction, each according to his own rhythm, but the need and its expression is seen in undisguised form in children.

But whether a child's need for stimulation is great or small, or whether his need for privacy is strong or weak, there is a considerable amount of stimulation in every child-parent relationship during the first six or so years of life. It is in the direction of the mother, for example, that a child usually smiles for the first time; it is upon the mother that a child depends for his survival; it is *vis-à-vis* the mother that a child learns the concept of "I" and "me." These are part of a child's needs for intimacy and closeness with his mother; but every child also has his own way of saying periodically — not only to his mother but to almost everyone else — "leave me alone."

As with other biologically-rooted behavior, the need for privacy has its developmental spurts, manifesting itself more strongly at different stages of development. Thus, after the early, criitical differentiation of the child's self from the mother, the need for privacy reasserts itself eruptively between the ages of 3 and 5 years, during the period that is often called "negativism." Its next major manifestation is during the first stage of puberty, when boys and girls tend to segregate themselves from each other and become shy with each other. This is also the time when children begin their fantasy-experiments with different role-identities. Following this evocation of the need for privacy is that of the second stage of puberty, when "the young person tends to isolate himself; from this time on, he will live with the members of his family as though with strangers."[16]

There are cultures that create intense overstimulation for their members, but at the same time they usually provide people with means for warding off excess stimulation and assume that they will be able to make maximal use of them. These means can be internal to the individual, as in Japanese culture,[17] or external institutionalized modes, such as the use of menstrual huts in some societies. Among the Athabascan Indians of the American northwest, for example, "the men could go off hunting by themselves, and thus weren't quite so vulnerable to 'cabin fever.' The women had their menstrual huts, and these provided the only real possibility of getting away from everything, because the children and other families were *always* around."[18] When cultures overstimulate their members intensely without providing means of warding off the excess excitation, it is possible to observe unrelieved extreme anxiety, as among the Kaingang of Brazil.[19]

The need for privacy is one of the motive forces in the individual's orientation to the world around him — that is, in the sub-system of the personality called the ego. More specifically, one of the functions of the ego is to control as needed the volume and intensity of stimulation from other people. Most people have the psychic equipment that enables them to make use of culturally appropriate ways of warding off stimulation when this need is felt, and to elicit it when stimulation is again needed. When employing the culturally appropriate means of reducing stimulation to a personally comfortable level — withdrawing, or saying "shut up" or "go away" without being insulting — or when inviting the resumption of such interaction, the individual continues to remain in contact with others. He is using a cultural mode of withdrawal which is also a patterned communication to others around him that he wishes to be free of stimulation and hopes that his need will be respected.

As a property of the ego, which is part of the individual's inherited equipment, the need for privacy can be seen most clearly in severely impaired states of the ego, as in schizophrenia.[20] The schizophrenic is a person who is born with (among other things) damaged psychic equipment for controlling stimulation by other people, especially by members of his nuclear family. He is unable to use the culturally appropriate modes for modulating the intensity of stimulation from other people and still remain in contact with them. Nevertheless, he must still cope with the problem. Partly as a result of this, he develops idiosyncratic and deculturalized modes of stimulus modulation: catatonic stupor (or outburst), a delusional system, megalomania, an isolated world of private fantasy and symbolism. He continues to maintain contact with others, but in a deculturalized manner that precludes true social communication.

In his divergent state, the schizophrenic teaches us what the non-schizophrenic is, and through this contrast illustrates the problem of maintaining privacy and modes of solving it. Thus, it has been observed that during extreme exacerbation of his pathology in the course of therapy, the schizophrenic requires absolute privacy; the therapist cannot speak directly to his patient, but must often avert his face and speak to him in the third person, as if to another person in the room. When he is able to face the therapist — and we need only consider the connotations of "facing" and "face" to grasp the significance of this — there has been improvement, and the patient can tolerate the invasion of his privacy by being addressed directly.[21]

Once the schizophrenic can master the problem of autonomously maintaining a degree of freedom from overstimulation in cultural rather than idiosyncratic fashion, he can resume participation in a social world of communication and symbolism. Thus, not only do people need to move toward each other but they must also move away from each other periodically in order to function effectively. But the techniques of doing so — and the ways in which these are learned — must be consonant with the institutional and value arrangements of the society. Menstrual huts and men's houses are incongruent with the structure of American institutions and values — a man's club is not his castle; it is only his temporary refuge — while separate bedrooms for spouses with locked doors under the same roof would not be consonant with the values and institutions of a polygamous society with extended families and lineages.

Part of a person's definition of himself, in addition to his anchorage in social space, is in his culturally provided techniques for maintaining a balance between approaching people and withdrawing from them. Just as every child needs to be fed, he must also develop a degree of certainty that when he is hungry he will be fed; just as every child needs physical and emotional warmth, he must also develop a degree of certainty that when he is cold he will be made warm.

Similarly, just as every child has a need for privacy, he must not only develop the sureness that he will be able to gratify this need when he has to, but he must also acquire the certainty that the people around him will not exceed permissible limits in their emotional contact with him at any one time. The individual can tolerate only a limited amount of any kind of stimulation — physical, sensory, or emotional — and no more.

Like any other bodily organ, the ego can suffer trauma; in connection with the ego, however, the notion of trauma is specific.

> The basic function of the mental apparatus is the re-establishment of stability after a disturbance by external stimuli. ... Whenever the maintenance of a (relative) equilibrium fails, a state of emergency arises. Too high an influx of excitement within the given unit of time is the simplest type of such an emergency. However, the expression 'too high' is a relative one; it means beyond the capacity of mastery. This capacity depends on constitutional factors as well as on all of the individual's previous experiences. There are stimuli of such overwhelming intensity that they have a traumatic effect on anyone. ... The ego may be regarded as having been developed for the purpose of avoiding [emotionally] traumatic states.[22]

Adults, of course, can satisfy the need for privacy more easily than children. But children, whose insularity is poorly developed, are more vulnerable to overwhelming emotional excitation. It is because of this that children often manifest a tendency to halt stimulation from other people suddenly

[170]

and completely, and acquire proficiency in slipping out of the physical or emotional grasp of others.

The satisfaction of children's basic biological needs is so important to their survival that society cannot leave them to fend for themselves; society must make provision for the satisfaction of these needs. In view of the importance of the need for privacy — for the development and maintenance of emotional separateness — consistent provision must be made for its gratification and training. I suggest that incest taboos are a social means of enabling people to maintain a necessary degree of privacy and emotional insularity within the family and other kinds of groups. These "other groups" will be discussed in Chapter 8.

Sexuality is the source of some of the strongest emotions. Incest taboos are a social way of saying to children, "You may go so far in your family relationships and no further; you have no need to fear that in your emotional closeness to your parents and siblings you will lose your identity in the overwhelming experience of sexual contact." Thereby, children are assured of objective as well as subjective separateness and emotional insularity.

Children need protection against seduction by all older people, and especially by members of their own families. Of course, the seduction of a child by a non-kinsman is psychologically and sociologically different from seduction by a member of the family, but in either event, "reaction to sexual stimulation can occur at all ages in the form appropriate to the child's development at the moment of seduction."[23] Thus, it makes a great difference by whom a child is seduced or with whom he engages in sexual play.

"Where inevitable seductions are concerned which occur among young children whenever they are unobserved . . . such events are harmless enough where they occur between partners who are on the same level of libidinal development. . . . It is different where a much younger child is exposed to sexual stimulation from an older one,"[24] to say nothing of such stimulation from an adult.

The ability of an individual to withstand consummate heterosexual relationships rests on the achievement of a degree of emotional maturity, or, as it is sometimes called, ego strength. I have said "withstand" because the biological endpoint — the consummation — of heterosexual intercourse is the state or experience of orgasm; this is an indivisible part of sexuality *per se.* An orgastic state is a potentially overwhelming experience in which there is a temporary loss of personal boundaries and of self. "This loss of the ego at the climax of sexual excitement is normally also the climax of the pleasure."[25] Thus, "it is only as young people emerge from their identity struggles that their egos can master . . . intimacy."[26]

The child's ego and modes of insularity are too weak to tolerate seduction by adults without severe pathological consequences. Sexual intercourse between emotionally involved individuals is much more intense than between emotionally uninvolved individuals, and this is probably true in all cultures. Hence, sexual relationships between a child and members of his family — the boundary-maintaining system which contains for him the most intense human emotions — would be most overwhelming for a child.

From a cross-cultural point of view, and from that of society, mature sexuality thus not only involves the ability to achieve and withstand heterosexual orgasm but it also involves the sociological placement of sexuality in relationships of fidelity, loyalty, and steadiness — as contrasted with promiscuity. It is for this reason that it is rare for societies to permit marriage before late adolescence. Prior to that time, the individual is still too immature to function effectively within an intense emotional-sexual relationship.

Reports of early marriage must be viewed with caution. Goode notes, for example, that "without doubt, the age at marriage is rising in all Arab countries; however, the general suppositions about marriage age for females in the past was probably as erroneous as that concerning the age of males. . . . There have always been *some* very early marriages in Arab countries, but *most* marriages took place at ages which would not have been thought improper in the West during the late nineteenth century, if we consider *average* rather than a few striking cases."[27] Similarly, he notes that in India, in cases of child marriage, "under the usual pattern, the girl returned to her parents' home after the marriage ceremony. She spent from one to several years there, until the *gauna* ceremony initiated the couple's cohabitation."[28] In the case of China, he observes: "At no time during the historical period has the ideal been 'child' marriage, if by that term we mean 'preadolescent.' The few data we possess from the past generation would suggest that child marriage was not *typical* in the past either."[29]

In somewhat different terms: the encapsulation of two individuals within a boundary-maintaining system increases their emotional involvement with each other. Because of this, most societies require that their members defer marriage until they are sufficiently mature emotionally to cope with the intense stimulation that is an integral part of sexuality within an institutionalized context. A society might permit pre-marital sexual intercourse rather freely to its adolescents, but the pre-marital relationship, unlike marriage, does not constitute a boundary-maintaining system.

I suggest that this emotional maturity stems largely from the development of the personality equipment that enables the individual to master the need for privacy. But we have also observed that different societies provide their members with different means for satisfying this need. Furthermore, since sexuality is most demanding of the ego and the need for privacy within the family (as a boundary-maintaining system), and since the society must take steps to protect the child from adult sexuality as a traumatic invasion of his privacy, we would logically expect to find the strictest curbs on sexuality within the family. Finally, if it is the family's characteristic as a boundary-maintaining system that is ultimately responsible for the establishment of sexual prohibitions — as contrasted with the family's characteristics as a kin group, as an economically cooperative unit, or as a reproductive and educative unit — then we should also expect to find that other boundary-maintaining systems also give rise to incest taboos.

EIGHT

BASES OF THE INCEST TABOO:
BOUNDARY-MAINTAINING SYSTEMS

A LTHOUGH incest taboos have their roots in the need for privacy, the two are not in one-to-one relationship; if they were, all sexual behavior would be taboo. Furthermore, since the need for privacy is part of the individual's sense of identity, and since the development of identity is closely tied to the institutional and value arrangements in a society, it is logical to expect that the ways in which an individual learns to satisfy his need for privacy will be closely tied to the society's institutional and value organization. And since the child's inchoate sexuality at the first stage of puberty requires that incest taboos be given their final inculcation at that point of development, we are also led to expect that the ways in which the incest taboo are taught are closely tied to the society's means of establishing a social-emotional identity.

To be specific, I suggest that societies that arrange their institutions around the values of sociological interdependence will make the final inculcation of the core incest taboo at the first stage of puberty by means of extrusion or brother-sister avoidance, or both. Conversely, societies that arrange their institutions around the values of sociological independence will make this final inculcation by means of verbal-symbolic instruction, while leaving the child within the boundaries of the nuclear family at the first stage of puberty. Furthermore, core and extensive incest taboos will occur in boundary-maintaining systems — specifically, those based on consanguineal kinship — since these social relationships are potentially the most threatening to the need for privacy.

Incest taboos arise in kin groups which have boundaries, that is, in consanguineal boundary-maintaining systems. Neither consanguinity nor the need for privacy alone gives rise to incest taboos. Rather, these prohibitions arise out of the confluence of the need for privacy with consanguinity as a boundary-maintaining system. Not all consanguineal kinship is localized within bounded groups. Thus, I am suggesting that incest taboos will not be found outside bounded kin groups.

When people are in very close cooperative contact with each other, whether in a nuclear family or between families, they must have limits set for them in their relationships with each other. They must know that no matter how much they cooperate, they cannot do so without limit. Thus, for example, even where people are expected to share their economic products, they do so within carefully prescribed limits.[1] Similarly, as we have seen in Chapter 6, all societies set stringent limits on the extent to which people can assume responsibility for each other's actions. The principal reason for this is that each family and every person must be assured of some degree of individuality and separateness from all others.

Boundary-maintaining consanguineal kin groups require great economic and other forms of cooperation, and they depend heavily on the values of inalienable social bonds. Relationships and feelings are strengthened as group-boundaries are solidified and as their members are encapsulated. People are bound together in such groups — sociologically, if not physically — regardless of how they feel about each other personally. The ethical imperatives of these groupings, with the attendant fears, guilts, and identifications characteristic of the memberships, are made up up of values of inalienability and extreme intimacy.*

When consanguineal relationships become boundary-maintaining systems, there ensues a contradiction between sexual contact within the group and the value of sociological interdependence. This contradiction also follows in other instances of extreme intimacy and institutionalization of relationships, as in the usual restriction of a man to only one "inalienable friend" in societies having this type of institutionalized friendship.[2] Some reasons for this contradiction will be elaborated after an analysis of the different types of incest taboos presented below. Before that, however, it is necessary to consider again some of the salient features of sociological boundary-maintaining systems.

A group becomes a boundary-maintaining system through the juxtaposition of two sets of pressures. One set comes from within the group, and such internal pressures vary from one type of group to another. The second set comes from without, usually — thought not always — from other groups.† Thus, a clan becomes a boundary-maintaining system as a result of pressures internal to it — the tendencies for people to cohere by the criteria of kinship, to establish patterns of land tenure, political organization, and religious

---

*As is well known, these values become deeply ingrained in the members of the society. For example, I found (in an unpublished cross-cultural study) that in most societies, the world of the dead is almost always a replica of the social organization of the world of the living.

†Pressures external to a group also come from its physical environment, such as those limiting its size and permanence of cohesion.

institutions commensurate with their levels of socio-cultural evolution, as well as from the expectations held of it by its component lineages and family groups. And a clan becomes a boundary-maintaining system as a result of pressures external to it — the presence of competing clans, the man-land ratio and other environmentally derived forces, national and supranational pressures, and the like.

It is in boundary-maintaining systems that people find their socio-emotional anchorage, and particular kinds of experiences are imposed by their socializers to help them find appropriate anchorages consonant with the society's goals. These experiences are pressures brought to bear on individuals, and these experiences, too, are part of the constellation of pressures of which sociological boundary-maintaining systems are made.

These pressures affect the individual as well as the group. It is because of this that all behavior takes place "within bounds" or "within the pale." One aspect of this circumscription of behavior is the fact that "no society allows for the random and promiscuous expression [of emotions or behavior] to just anyone. Rather, one may communicate these feelings, either verbally, physically, or materially only to certain people."[3] Anchorage within a sociological boundary-maintaining system creates stronger feelings of closeness among its members than placement in a group which is not a boundary-maintaining system. Since consanguinity *per se* usually produces stronger feelings among people than do other types of relationships, a boundary-maintaining system composed of consanguineal kinsmen would lead to stronger feelings of closeness among its members than a boundary-maintaining system that is composed of non-consanguineal kinsmen. Therefore, since institutionalized limits on behavior become more necessary as their closeness with each other increases, we would logically expect these limits to be strongest in boundary-maintaining systems based on biological kinship.

In attempting to relate incest taboos to the need for privacy and to kinship systems, the core taboos — those of the nuclear family — have to be seen as made up of two sets of taboos. These differ from each other in temporal rather than structural terms. The first are the taboos that prohibit the sexual initiative of parents toward their children; they do not apply to the child, because he is impotent. The second apply to the children, and their final inculcation takes place at the first stage of puberty.* The first set of core taboos — temporally speaking — are one of the institutional modes assuring that parents will not exceed limits in contacts with their children. The second set of taboos — those which take effect after puberty — are an institutionalized limitation on the extent to which people can go in their emotional interaction within a boundary-maintaining system.†

---

*These taboos are surely being taught continuously in all societies, but this is different from their final inculcation.

†I think it is my focus on the temporal dimension as well as on the boundary-maintaining quality of kin groups which have incest taboos, that led me to such different conclusions from Aberle *et al.* 1963. Specifically, they are unable by their analysis to explain the extensions of the incest taboo to the wider kin group. Nor can they explain why the brother-sister taboo is more important in matrilineal society then in others; this problem was discussed in Schneider and Gough (1961, 12-3) and will be discussed more fully below. If it is indeed true, as Aberle *et al.* claim, that the taboos solve the problem of sexual competition and genetic inbreeding, why does it appear that the mother-son taboo is more important than the father-daughter taboo, even though there cannot be mother-son reproduction for many years? Granted that the genetic problem does exist, could not the solution to the genetic problem be an accidental off-shoot of other reasons for the taboo rather than an intended or purposeful solution?

(1) *Mother-son incest taboo*. Mother-son incest almost always and automatically suggests the presence of psychosis in one or both persons involved (at least in Western society).* One of the criteria of sexual maturity is the development of a sense of self that is separate from the mother's. Mother-son incest suggests that such differentiation has not taken place and that the two are still in psychological fusion and symbiosis.

It is apparently meaningless from a physiological point of view, however, to prohibit a woman from engaging in such activity with her pre-pubertal (and impotent) son. A simple "learning" explanation of this phenomenon, one that says that the post-pubertal taboo must be learned at an early age in order to be effective, is insufficient. Such learning is, of course, necessary, but it does not explain the universality of the pre-pubertal taboo. This universality suggests that there is something in the constitution of the child — regardless of the society to which he belongs — that makes a taboo on mother-son incest necessary even before the child is capable of heterosexual activity.

As a result of the investigations of Jean Piaget and of psychoanalytic investigators, it is known that the thought processes and logical axioms of children are different from those of adults. The thinking of the child is largely syncretistic, in his tendency to equate wish and deed, to assume

---

*For the reasoning underlying this suggestion and for its wide acceptance among clinicians, see Mahler 1952. Neither father-daughter (see Weinberg 1955) nor sibling incest is so automatically suggestive of psychosis, at least in Western society, paralleling the fact that the sibling relationship (except in matrilineal societies, see below) and father-daughter relationships are never as intense as mother-child relationships and never involve the fusion and symbiosis normal to the early mother-child relationship.

that wish leads directly to action, and in the fact that "he does not distinguish between external and internal, subjective and objective."[4] Juxtaposing these facts with the universality of the taboo on incest between mother and pre-pubertal son, the prohibition appears to be a defense for the pre-pubertal boy against the syncretism of incestuous wish and deed. That is, the boy has to know that his wished action cannot be carried out because it is forbidden. If society left the mother-son incest taboo only at the level of pre-pubertal impotence, too many children would be traumatized by the anxiety resulting from the irrational conviction that they had, indeed, engaged in incest with their mother. Adults, drawing on their repressed past, say, "The wish is father to the deed;" in the axiom of childhood logic, on the other hand, "Wish equals deed."

Furthermore, and perhaps more important, the explicit injunction on mother-son sexuality provides parent and child with a formalized awareness of the intergenerational separateness that is part of the boundary system of every family. This institutionalized division within the family is one of the salient features of its boundary-maintaining system, with respect to which the child is manipulated in the course of developing a sense of identity. Since mature emotional identification is never complete, and since such identification requires a measure of separateness and insularity, the institutionally imposed separateness between the generations within the family is also in the service of establishing emotional identification and a sense of identity.

The fact that women in some societies manipulate their sons' genitalia, make overt castration threats, and indulge in varieties of mock sexual play, does not contradict the notion of the threat of trauma in adult-child sexual relationships. None of these activities involves intromission. Furthermore, it would be surprising if careful psychological investigation among such people did not reveal that these experiences left permanent emotional scars on the child.

(2) *Father-daughter incest taboo.* The problems giving rise to the father-daughter incest taboo are different from those leading to the mother-son taboo, although they share some commonalities. The difference, of course, is that a man is able to force or seduce his daughter into sexual relations, whereas a woman cannot do so with her son.

The significance of the latter lies in the trauma and psychological devastation that would result for a young girl through incestuous relations with her father. The degree of damage to the girl may not be as great as might result from mother-son incest, since father and daughter are normally not as close and symbiotic in relationship as mother and son, but there would be trauma for the girl, nevertheless. The source of this danger is twofold. The first stems from the nature of sexuality and its relationship to the psychic structure. The second has to do with the nature of boundary-maintaining sub-systems within the boundary-maintaining system of the nuclear family.[5]

(a) Since the implied end point of heterosexual behavior involves, in part, a momentary loss of personal boundaries, and since the loss of personal boundaries is especially frightening to the immature (in its threat of loss of identity), children must be protected from this overwhelming experience. In French, for example, the term for orgasm is "la petite morte."

Why is not sexual contact between father and pre-pubertal daughter simply subsumed under the rubric of seduction or "molestation" of a minor (or the equivalent), and why is the sexual contact of father and post-pubertal daughter also forbidden?

Relationships within the nuclear family, especially during the earliest years of a child's vulnerability, are intimate and intense. The earliest and most important emotional iden-tifications of a child take place within the nuclear family. The emotional maturity necessary for consummate sexual behavior stems, in part, from the individual's awareness — not necessarily conscious — that in adulthood he will be able to flee emotionally, or satisfy his need for privacy when nec-essary. Children do not have such an awareness. Hence, they need institutionalized protection against those who might be attracted to them sexually. The taboo is continued beyond puberty as an institutionalized representation of the continued need for insularity from consanguineal members of the bounded family group.

(b Within the family as a boundary-maintaining system are at least two sub-systems that are demarcated generation-ally. Parents — who meet and court each other as strangers, people who have not grown up together within the same boundary-maintaining kin group — have different mutual interests, needs, responsibilities, involvements and goals than their children. These are pressures giving rise to a set of boundaries that demarcate the parents, not only from all other couples and families, but especially from their chil-dren. The children are themselves differentiated from their parents by their own boundaries. Thus, for example chil-dren easily unite in defiance of their parents, in mutual con-spiracy, as pressure groups, and so forth.

One of the functions of parent-child incest taboos is to keep children out of the marital boundary-maintaining system so that their parents can maintain necessary identifications with each other. Father-daughter incest would severely blur a girl's identity as a daughter, for it would threaten to erase the complementary inter-generational boundary systems. Furthermore, since the maintenance of authority — one of the requisites of any family system — depends largely on status boundaries, as well as upon social and emotional distance, parent-child incest would remove this distance and would make the family authority pattern almost impossible to maintain.[6]

(3) *Brother-sister incest taboo.* The brother-sister relationship varies in importance among societies, at least as far as institutional and value arrangements are concerned, but it can be surmised from the reports of ethnographers that brother-sister incest occurs more frequently than mother-son or father-daughter incest. But this taboo is no less important than the other two, though brother-sister incest is a much more serious offense in a matrilineal society than in a patrilineal or bilateral society.

Brother and sister normally grow up in intimate and intense emotional relationship; furthermore, they are members of the same boundary-maintaining system and sub-system within the family. As a result, the taboo on sexual contact between them is necessary to maintain emotional separateness and insularity.

However, a comparison of different descent systems reveals that the brother-sister relationship is different in matrilineal systems than in others. As Schneider has pointed out:

Bases of the Incest Taboo: Boundary-Systems

Let us take as a given feature of the descent groups with which we are concerned the prohibition of sexual relations between brother and sister. Patrilineal descent is consistent with the demands of this incest taboo in a way that matrilineal descent is not. In the patrilineal case a woman's sexual and reproductive activities are the primary concern of her husband and her husband's group, and not of her brother. In this sense there is a consistency between the prohibition against sexual interest between brother and sister and the locus of concern with a woman's sexual and reproductive activities. On the other hand, in matrilineal descent groups a woman bears children who perpetuate her own and her brother's group, and her sexual and reproductive activities are a matter of direct concern for her brother — although she is a tabooed sexual object for him. [Thus], *in matrilineal descent groups there is an element of potential strain in the fact that the sister is a tabooed sexual object for her brother, while at the same time her sexual and reproductive activities are a matter of interest to him.*"[7]

This strain makes the brother-sister incest taboo more important (psychologically and sociologically) in a matrilineal system than in any other, and produces greater rigidity of the taboo in such societies than in others.

There is merit in the notion of "greater temptation leading to greater repression"; even more suggestive, however, is Schneider's formulation of the consistency between patrilineal descent and the brother-sister incest taboo. The formality or systematization of descent systems is one thing, while the reality of everyday relationships is another. There are many possible permutations and combinations between the rule of descent and geographical relationship. For example, adult brother and sister in a matrilineal society might live

[185]

several miles apart, while in a patrilineal society they might live only a few yards away from each other.

It is here that we can observe the overriding significance of the concept of sociological boundary-maintaining systems in the establishment of incest taboos. Schneider's hypothesis of the consistency between patrilineal — and even bilateral — descent and brother-sister incest taboos can be carried one step further by suggesting that the consistency and lesser degree of strain between patrilineal descent and the brother-sister incest taboo results from the fact that the sexual and reproductive activities of siblings of different sex are in the interests of different, and sometimes competing, boundary-maintaining descent groups, since their respective children will be members of different groups. Similarly, there is potentially greater strain in the brother-sister incest taboo in a matrilineal society because — although both are tabooed to each other sexually — the sister's sexual and reproductive activities take place within and in the interests of her brother's descent group, a boundary-maintaining group that is often in competitve relationship with her husband's group.

Thus, the nuclear family provides several parallel situations with sufficient variation between them to support the hypothesis that core incest taboos arise out of the juxtaposition of the need for privacy with consanguinity as a boundary-maintaining system. The three core taboos arise within situations of extreme intimacy that must be counteracted to meet the need for privacy; at the same time, each is a response to a unique problem within the family.

(4) *Extensive incest taboos.* The extension of incest ta-

[186]

boos beyond the nuclear family into the wider kin group has been the major stumbling block in attempts to understand the universality of incest taboos, especially because these taboos are not, on the surface, alike in every society. However, the analysis of the three taboos in the nuclear family suggests that more uniformity exists in these extensions than is apparent. The three core taboos suggest that incest taboos will be found outside the nuclear family when consanguineal kinsmen are anchored together within a boundary-maintaining system. These are the extensive incest taboos.

Unilineal societies almost always have at least one type of descent group that is bounded physically or socially, and sometimes in both ways. It is an accepted anthropological principle that the non-articulating line of descent is extremely important in unilineal societies *vis-à-vis* the articulating line.[8] Thus, to cite but one example, the matrilineal Hopi say that a person "belongs" to the matrilineal kin group but is a "child" of his father's kin. And while he has one set of reciprocal relationships with his matrilineal kin, he has a different set of such relationships with his paternal kin.

One of the most important pressures that enables a consanguineal kin group to function as a boundary-maintaining system is the presence of other similarly constituted groups; these serve as one set of external pressures. In other words, in order for any group to exist, it must have at least one other similarly constituted group alongside. The existence of two or more bounded groups will give rise to parallel boundary-maintaining systems; to be specific, the existence of one clan is partially responsible for the existence of other clans and *vice versa*. This suggests further that a patrilineal system of descent will, as a set of pressures, give rise to its obverse (maternal) line of descent as an articulating sociological principle, and that the two in juxtaposition enable each other to operate as separate but complementary boundary-maintaining systems.

Thus, it follows logically that when a patrilineal kin group is strongly bounded, the maternal line will be under pressure to constitute a boundary-maintaining system, although of a different sort than the patrilineal line. The more this maternal group functions as a boundary-maintaining system the greater the tendency for it, too, to establish incest taboos. This is apparently why many unilineal societies extend their incest taboos bilaterally. Thus, Murdock noted that "the direction of the extension of incest taboos is determined primarily by the presence of consanguineal kin groups."[9] Similarly, he found that "non-extension [is associated with] the absence or unreported presence of all consanguineal kin groups."[10] In addition to structural factors, Murdock also stressed the importance of time in making such extensions possible.[11] This does not contradict the hypothesis of reciprocal pressures between groups in establishing boundary-maintaining systems; instead, it complements it. Pressures that form sociological boundary-maintaining systems require time to make themselves felt. Considerably more research will be needed to understand this phenomenon, and until such research is carried out, Murdock's cross-cultural data on the extensions of the incest taboo[12] can be taken as support for the hypotheses suggested here.

The conclusions derived from the analysis of the three core taboos and their extensions can be stated as a general principle about all social relationships: *In examining any social bond — dyadic, triadic, or larger — it is not only necessary to find the factors that make it possible for people to approach each other or that interfere with such proximity, but it is equally important to learn whether any insulating or distance-maintaining mechanisms have been provided so that individuals can modulate the stimulation impinging on them, in the service of the need for privacy.*

When consanguineal kinsmen are not encapsulated within a boundary-maintaining kin group, they therefore retain an element of separateness from each other. Thus, for example, partners in a cross-cousin marriage usually come from different boundary-maintaining kin groups. Cross-cousin marriage is usually found in unilineal societies. Homans and Schneider have shown that matrilateral cross-cousin marriage tends to take place in patrilineal societies while patrilateral cross-cousin marriage tends to take place in matrilineal societies.[13] In other words, unilineal descent groups remain fully exogamous even when there is cross-cousin marriage and these cross cousins retain their sense of socio-emotional anchorage in their respective kin groups.

However, when kinsmen are encapsulated within a boundary-maintaining kin group, they live with a strong degree of solidarity — as in societies that base their institutional arrangements on the value of sociological interdependence — and must have institutional means for the maintenance of privacy. One of the ways in which this is accomplished in the kinship sphere is through the incest taboo, by the implied dictum: "You and everyone else in the group can go only so far in your relationships with each other, but no further."

In a bounded patrilineal kin group, cooperation usually takes place among the men. But incest taboos refer to *heterosexual* relationships. Since it is the men who are welded together into cooperating groups, it is they who need the institutional modes for maintaining privacy from each other. How do incest taboos help them in this connection?

Here again, as in understanding the core taboos, the concept of boundary-maintaining systems emerges as indispensable. The goal of the incest taboo as a means of maintaining privacy is achieved by compelling the members of the kin group to find their sexual partners elsewhere — beyond the boundaries of the consanguineal kin group. I suggest that this is sufficient to provide the members of the group with a necessary degree of privacy within a boundary-maintaining system that is based on consanguineal (inalienable) ties. This rule of exogamy is an emotional removal from the boundary-maintaining system, in much the same fashion as extrusion and brother-sister avoidance are removals from the boundary-maintaining system of the nuclear family. In the case of consanguineal kin groups however, this often appears to be more than a removal of sexuality from within the bounds of a kin group. It can sometimes be thought of as a kind of "emotional slumming," in which the sexuality is displaced to a group competitive with one's own and one that can even be held in extremely low regard. Thus, it would appear that in many societies there is not only the assurance that privacy will be maintained in the context of extreme intimacy and cooperation but that it will also be displaced to a member of a group with which there are no such ties.

The entire process of socialization of sexuality is based

on the displacement of sexuality from within boundary-maintaining systems, first from the family and then from the kin group.* Since the establishment of a social and emotional anchorage also requires physical manipulation of the child in relation to the boundaries of the nuclear family and the kin group — either by disrupting his relationships to his family or by leaving them undisturbed — the inculcation of the rules of exogamy and of a sense of anchorage are parts of a single process.

The climactic establishment of the incest taboo is achieved by the same means that are used to establish a social-emotional anchorage and a sense of identity.† In societies in which children are being brought up for sociological interdependence, the incest taboo will be given its final inculcation by extrusion or brother-sister avoidance, or both.

These customs serve as prototypes for the more generalized rule that sexuality must be removed from within the sociological boundary-maintaining systems in which the individual is to be anchored. Such profoundly disruptive experiences climax several years of listening to adults' discussions of relationships between descent groups in terms of the rules of exogamy and marriage arrangements; of hearing ribald discussions of tabooed, permitted, and preferred marriage relationships in men's houses and in similar contexts; and of learning the sexual relevance of one's social map from peers and socializers.

It is in these terms that we can understand the sexual fac-

---

*The universal engraftment of the rule of exogamy on sexuality might help, in part, to explain the prevalence of adultery.

†This suggestion cannot be verified by the data available, but it is offered here on the strength of the regularities and parallels that have been observed and discussed thus far.

tor underlying extrusion and brother-sister avoidance that is indicated by its termination at marriage. Marriage does more than provide acceptable sexual relationships in lieu of incestuous ones; it marks the final and complete removal of sexuality from the boundary-maintaining system in which one is anchored, into an entirely new boundary-maintaining relationship: the marital.* It is required in every society that the symbols of sexuality, its subjective meanings, and its proprieties be placed within a boundary-maintaining system other than the consanguineal group within which the individual finds his anchorage.

In view of the relationship between the inculcation of the incest taboo and experiences in the first stage of puberty in societies that bring up their children for sociological interdependence, is there a relationship between initiation ceremonies of the second stage and cultural attitudes toward premarital sexual intercourse?[14] The data show (see Table 9) that there is no relationship between the presence or absence of these rites de passage and attitudes toward premarital sexual behavior.

Transitional rites, where they are practiced, delineate the adolescent's social status with much greater clarity than in societies that do not perform them. But heterosexual intercourse, whether before marriage or after, is an entirely different kind of experience than the recognition of social status

*I think this is what Linton meant in his observation (1942, 597) that marriage is "also a rite de passage relative to the age-sex system. A first marriage transfers the participants from the child or adolescent to the adult category." This is also the fundamental error in psychoanalytic thinking which equates incest with Oedipus, and sees it and the taboos on it as nothing more than Oedipus. It can be suggested on the basis of the present research that Oedipus is but a special case of events which transpire within the broad realm of boundary-maintaining systems.

Table 9

Relationships between Experiences at the Second Stage of
Puberty and Cultural Rules Concerning
Premarital Sexual Relationships*

	Premarital Sexual Relationships Permitted	Premarital Sexual Relationships Prohibited
Initiation Ceremonies Practiced	12	7
No Initiation Ceremonies Practiced	27	13
	$X^2 = 1.24$	$p < .75$

*There are no data for six societies.

or of social-emotional anchorage. Intercourse involves personal and body boundaries, in addition to the most intense sensations, and thus requires a much more profound preparation than can be provided for in the relatively brief experience of an initiation ceremony.

We have seen that the tendency to anchor the individual in the kin group is stronger in societies that possess unilineal descent groups, but the presence of these groupings is not a guarantee that such anchorage will take place. Similarly, it is possible to anchor the individual within a bilateral kindred, although this is unusual.

It is important to an understanding of incest taboos to recognize that all societies possess boundary-maintaining kin groups of one type or another. Although not all societies use these groups as points of anchorage for their members, it is in these that incest taboos are always located. When societies practice extrusion or brother-sister avoidance, they coincidentally exploit these means of securing anchorage in the wider kin group for the inculcation of the core incest taboos. The values of sociological interdependence are not the reasons for the existence of incest taboos, either in the nuclear family or in the wider kin group; but these values are inculcated in ways that are also used for implanting the core taboos. In societies in which the individual is anchored in the nuclear family, the core taboos must be inculcated by means of verbal instruction and by other symbolic communications. Extensive taboos are always implanted verbally.

Whereas boundary-maintaining kin groups generally have stronger boundaries and encompass many more areas of feeling and activity than do the looser kindreds of bilateral societies, the latter are also boundary-maintaining systems which impose reciprocal obligations and privileges. Unilineal groups and kindreds have different boundary-systems because they emerge out of different pressures, but both are boundary-maintaining kin groups.[15] The stronger the encapsulation of members of bilateral kindreds, the greater the tendency to extend incest taboos into them. Thus, as the bilateral kindred has lost significance in most segments of American society, especially in terms of reciprocal obligations and privileges, the weaker have become the taboos on marriage within those kindreds, especially between cousins.

In societies in which neither extrusion nor brother-sister avoidance is practiced, as noted, reliance must be placed on verbal or other symbolic means of inculcating the core taboos. Verbal instruction in these taboos certainly occurs in all societies, but this means is exclusive in some societies, while use can be made of extrusion or brother-sister avoidance in combination with verbal instruction in other societies. In the former, there is continuity in the child's physical relationship with his nuclear family; but the core taboo must still be implanted, in view of the child's impending heterosexuality. I suggest that even in the absence of physical discontinuities, there is still an *emotional* discontinuity in the child's relationship to his family, and that this has two sources. The first is the child's tendency to become shy in the presence of the opposite sex and for boys and girls to segregate themselves from each other. These are alternatives to extrusion and brother-sister avoidance, emphasized by the children themselves, in order to maintain the insularity and separateness that they need in the face of incipient and confusing sexuality. To reiterate, children do not have the psychological means for meeting the need for privacy autonomously and for setting limits for themselves, except in the grossest forms of approach and withdrawal. It is not until after the second stage of puberty has passed that the confusions of nascent sexuality begin to abate and the children can develop the culturally approved gradations along continua of approach and withdrawal.

The second source of this emotional discontinuity lies with the child's parents; there are no observations of which I am aware to support this and I am stating it as an hypothesis that could be investigated by empirical research. I suspect that in societies that practice neither extrusion nor brother-sister avoidance, the parents alter their relationships to the children at some point during the first stage of puberty by possibly becoming slightly distant, by setting new limits, by imposing new expectations, by giving them new names or nicknames, and the like. These changes in parental behavior might be geared to parents' attempts to cope with their own conflicts over their children's nascent sexuality, or they might be preconscious attempts on the parents' part to meet their children's new needs.

In either case, where extrusion or brother-sister avoidance are practiced, these are physical means that enable the child to find an anchorage, a sense of identity, and modes of privacy — especially sexual privacy — at the confusing first stage of puberty. Where these customs are absent, symbolic social means must be employed. The need for privacy is the genetic basis of the incest taboos; boundary-maintaining consanguinity is the social factor that determines where incest taboos will occur in the nuclear family and in its wider kinship space.

PART III

NINE

METHODOLOGY:
MECHANICAL AND THEORETICAL

T HE procedures used in the present investigation have made themselves apparent, but I would like now to speak about some of the mechanics of cross-cultural research in detail. Later, I will speak of some of its theoretical aspects.

There are different approaches to cross-cultural research.[1] A considerable number of published investigations have, to varying extents, employed the facilities of the Cross-Cultural Files at Yale University. In recent years, these facilities have been made available in several areas of the United States, and have since become known as the Human Relations Area Files. The procedures and some of the rationale of the Files are presented in the introductory sections of *Outline of Cultural Materials*[2] and in Murdock's publications[3] on some of the research methods that can be employed in using the Files.

The present study is one of a series. The first was a cross-cultural inquiry into the problem of why people share or do not share their food and money in pre-literate and folk societies.[4] I tested my hypothesis for this study — or, more accurately, for one part of it — in these Files. This procedure had to be abandoned during the second phase of the research, and the results were illuminating. I shall return to this experience later. The second study in the series dealt with "Patterns of Friendship."[5] There are others, not yet published.

Several studies of initiation ceremonies have been made in recent years,[6] and my fundamental disagreements with almost all of them are partly theoretical and conceptual, and partly of a methodological nature. The theoretical disagreements will be treated elsewhere;[7] I will deal with the methodological problems in this chapter. Since the other studies of initiation ceremonies have used the facilities of the Human Relations Area Files, I will orient the discussion in this chapter around that tool of cross-cultural research.

I did not use the Human Relations Area Files for the study presented in this book, but only complete ethnographic and field reports. From a previously selected sample of societies and communities throughout the world, I read, in their entirety, the reports on each culture. Data relevant to the problem of "the sense of responsibility" were marked off and typewritten verbatim onto file cards, usually by a secretary who did not know the hypotheses for the study. These cards were filed alphabetically by cultural groups or units, and the process repeated for each of the separate parts of the study. In all of the cross-cultural studies I have carried out thus far, this procedure had to be repeated several times because of the omission of relevant variables in my original working hypotheses. I had to continue reading until I had collected all the necessary data for the problem on which I was working. But more about this, too, below.

I began this series of cross-cultural investigations with the hope of achieving a truly random and representative sample of the world's societies. The criteria that I originally established for myself in this connection were twofold. First, each culture had to be an independent unit, that is, unrelated to any other culture or society. Second, I intended to work with a proportionate sampling of societies in each culture area. This criterion had to be abandoned very early in my research on the problem of food sharing.

All of the cross-cultural investigations that I have conducted have been based on the same basic sample of societies. In testing the hypotheses for the study of behavior with respect to food distribution, I required three sets of data: those reporting the experiences of infants and children in connection with feeding, those dealing with the behavior of adults with respect to food and money, and those covering patterns of settlement and kinship. I had to abandon my second criterion — the random sampling of each culture area — because very few ethnographic reports contain all these data. I had also hoped that the reports for the societies in my sample would include data with respect to toilet training. If I had insisted on this, I would have ended with an even smaller sample.

After completing the study of food sharing and turning to the problem of patterns of friendship, I had to consider the question of sampling procedures more directly than in the first inquiry, and decide whether to retain the sample used in the first investigation or select a new sample that would be more representative of the distribution of societies. I elected the first alternative — that is, to continue with the original sample — because of my long-range goals in these investigations.

More rigorous sampling methods for each of my studies might have given me sharper insights into the problems with which I was dealing. But if I had accepted the requirements of random sampling more strictly, and if I had worked with entirely different selections of societies in each of the studies, I would have done so at the expense of broader interests and theoretical considerations. Sampling methods, like any other procedures of research, can be made ends in themselves, or they can be used as expedient instruments for achieving other goals. The vehicles we press into service and by which we arrive at a destination are always dictated by the conditions under which we use them.

In brief, my selection of societies for these cross-cultural studies was originally determined by the requirements of certain minimal data for the study of food-distribution. An attempt was made to locate representative cultures for each culture area within the limits imposed by the required data. Important in connection with the present study is the fact that regularities and consistencies in the data have appeared so strikingly in a sample that was originally selected for an entirely different problem.

An investigator in cross-cultural research, or any other inquiry for that matter, can be sorely tempted to "find" or "interpret" data to substantiate his own hypotheses. One way of "solving" this problem in cross-cultural research, as attempted by Whiting and Child,[8] is to have the data rated by a series of independent observers who do not know the hypotheses, and then derive a composite score from all the independent ratings. In conversations among anthropologists and sociologists, this seems increasingly to be considered standard and desirable procedure.

Parallel with ideals, however, exists reality. And one of the inexorable facts of the reality of modern science is that research costs money, often in large quantities. By reason of financial circumstance I have conducted my own cross-cultural research in all of my investigations, including the one reported here.

Since the danger of bias in the judgment of other people's data is great I felt that, in the absence of independent ratings, the most feasible procedure would be to state my hypotheses as clearly as possible and to report the data themselves in such a way that the hypotheses would then stand or fall directly on these data. Thus, I have tried to present the results of all these investigations, including the present one, so as to allow anyone else to "repeat the experiment," using the data that I have used or testing my hypotheses using entirely different sets of data. That is why I presented the data as reported in Chapters 4, 5, and 6.

As for the problem of the interpretation of the data, I have attempted, as far as possible, to remove the very possibility of interpreting or misinterpreting the facts. I feel that although there are a considerable number of hypotheses in this study, they are still sufficiently few in number, and they are stated in explicit behavioral terms. In colloquial language, I have attempted to formulate these hypotheses strictly in terms of "do societies act as I have suggested in my hypotheses or don't they?"

At this point, I would like to discuss some of my own experiences with the Human Relations Area Files. My purpose here is not to deny or discredit the usefulness of these Files, but to point to apparent limitations in them. I am going to discuss this in the light of two of my cross-cultural investigations, the first and the most recent, although I have had much the same experience with several other studies.

In the first cross-cultural study, my original hypothesis dealt with the relationships between early feeding experiences and adult behavior in the distribution of food. At the time that I formulated this hypothesis, I tested it in these Files. The data substantiated the hypothesis, and the results were reported as part of my doctoral dissertation.[9]

While doing that research, however, I noted that there seemed to be different degrees of food-sharing, that is, peo-ple in some societies shared more than people in other groups. But there was nothing in my hypothesis to account for this difference in degrees of sharing, so I grouped all societies together, in the belief that "sharing" constituted a single generic cultural category, and that individual societies elaborated on this pattern for a variety of undetermined reasons. In other words, I had a hypothesis that contained a "one-to-one" relationship, and the data seemed to substan-tiate it. Now I have learned that such a "one-to-one" relation-ship is generally suspect.

A short time later, I wanted to continue this research but, living in a different city, I did not have access to the Files. I did, however, have access to an excellent ethnographic li-brary and resumed the research using complete ethno-graphic reports. In the course of this phase of the investiga-tion, I began to realize that the "variations" in degrees of

sharing were other than mere cultural elaborations of a generic pattern. They turned out to be discrete phenomena or
patterns, representing separate and distinct principles of organization that had to be accounted for by factors not present in my original hypothesis. This realization led me to
abandon the data I had already collected, and to begin the
research again, using only complete ethnographic reports.

Along with my "hunch" that different degrees of sharing actually reflected different economic and social systems, another factor began to suggest itself repeatedly: that these
different systems had some relationship to spatial dis-
tances between households. From this, other variables dealing with relationships between households, especially temporal, began to build into a pattern, until I felt that I could
more adequately explain sharing and non-sharing in fairly
complete terms. The important point here is that I am certain that these relationships would not have been uncovered
had I confined my research to the Files. This, of course, may
indicate a lack in my own theoretical equipment, but I doubt
that this alone would account for the experience.

Another side of this problem is empirical, though no less
an intuitive or subjective aspect of cross-cultural research.
Simpson has observed that one "feature that distinguishes
science from other fields of thought and of activity is that it
is self-testing by the same kinds of observations from which
it arises and to which it applies. It is, to use a currently popu-
lar but perhaps overworked bit of jargon, a cybernetic system with a feedback that in spite of oscillations keeps its
orientation as nearly as may be toward reality."[10] Hypotheses about cultural events or patterns have to be derived from

the very data by which they are to be tested. This can some-times be accomplished by using the Files, depending, of course, on the nature of the problem. But there are in-numerable instances in which an investigator can search for a particular datum in a most obvious category in the Files and not find it. He may then assume that this custom is ab-sent in the societies examined or that it missed the attention of the ethnographer — but neither of these need be the case.

In beginning research for this book, I conducted a "test run" of my original hypotheses in the Files to learn whether there was any foundation in fact for some of my ideas. It turned out to be completely fruitless. Fortunately, however, I obeyed an intuition that my first hypotheses were nonethe-less useful, and guided by earlier experiences, decided to do the research anyway using complete ethnographic sources.

Had I used the cross-cultural Files for this research, I would naturally have sought some of my data under the cate-gories having to do with "socialization," child-rearing cus-toms, and kinship relationships. In about one-fifth of the societies in my sample, the data that one would normally ex-pect to find in these categories actually come from sections in ethnographies labeled "material culture," from photo-graphs, and from maps or diagrams of settlement patterns. In other instances, the data I needed were in sections that had almost nothing to do with the upbringing of children. One of the societies in the sample, for instance, is represented in the published literature by only one monograph and this is devoted almost exclusively to the ways in which children are brought up. In seeking to learn whether there is extrusion or brother-sister avoidance in that group, I found these data in a census presented in a brief introduction to the book. In another case my data were found in a phrase within a sentence: "Since children leave their parents' home at about the age of ten to live elsewhere. . . ." Often, the role of kinsmen in rearing children was mentioned briefly in sections of reports that had nothing to do with kinship relationships or with the rearing of children. The point that I want to stress is that even though an attempt is made in the Files to present such "buried" data, this is not done consistently and successfully. When one relies on the Files to conduct his research, therefore, he is actually relying on someone else for the crucial first stage, and he is using data edited for him in advance.

I have gone into some details in this connection, instead of leaving this line of thought to be shared with colleagues informally, because they indicate a limitation in the use of the Files. Hypotheses, or statements of relationships and correlations, as suggested earlier, must emerge from the very data by which these hypotheses are to be tested. Eventually, as the number of cultures included in the Files is increased, it will be possible to test such hypotheses in greater breadth than is now possible. Thus, for example, one could select a representative sample of fifty or seventy-five cultures from Murdock's[11] sample of 400 cultures in order to derive and formulate hypotheses. After this preliminary small sample has been exhausted in complete ethnographic reports, the investigator could then test his hypotheses against the remainder of the sample of 400 by using the Files. At the same time, however, it should always be borne in mind that the quality of the Files is as good as the data included in them. Thus, nothing in the Files can overcome the omission of factual information.

The question of when one can leave off reading hundreds of books and articles several times over for a single investigation and turn to the Files for speedier results is legitimate, and I do not think there is any definite answer beyond the one suggested in the previous paragraph. Perhaps others will be forthcoming from other cross-cultural investigators. As those who have been most intimately associated with the Files have cautioned: "The files are intended as an aid to research in the human sciences, not as a substitute for other types of research."[12] Whiting, in his discussion of methodology of cross-cultural research, orients his formulations almost exclusively to the organization of the Files. Despite this, however, his statement can also be applied to this kind of comparative research in general: "the cross-cultural method, although it is still in its infancy, shows promise of being a useful adjunct to other research methods designed for the development of a general science of human behavior."[13] It is quite probable that the Files are best suited for inquiry into certain kinds of problems, while the use of complete reports — either exclusively or in conjunction with the Files — is best suited for others.

Readers may question the inclusion in my sample of the Midlanders (my name for modern mid-western Americans) and the Shtetl, the socially isolated Jewish community of eastern Europe prior to the German cannibalistic psychosis. They have been included for several reasons, two of which are especially important to me. First, I want to underscore the point that anthropologists and sociologists do not ordinarily study societies. They usually study individual communities, because almost all societies are too large for direct observation. And we investigate the ways of life in communities, not as ends in themselves, but to learn about the workings of culture and social structure.

When an anthropologist investigates a community in a pre-literate society, for example, he is often proceeding on the assumption that this particular community is more or less representative of the total society. He knows that no two communities are identical, but he assumes that the processes and principles underlying the pattern of living are pretty much the same in most of the communities of the society. In that sense, he is taking one segment as a sample of the total society.

One of the things that makes communities comparable for purposes of cross-cultural research is that all communities have boundaries. Some boundary-systems are more distinct than others, while some are very vague and poorly defined, whether they be social or physical boundaries. We know very little as yet about the processes involved in social boundary-systems, about how they are maintained, and about their deeper functions. But it is known that most social life takes place within community boundaries and other social boundary-systems.

Thus, whenever I compare communities with respect to a particular problem — such as the sense of responsibility — there is always the idea in the back of my mind that I am comparing boundary-systems. I am aware that I can only compare boundary-systems that are of the same order. Thus,

I cannot compare a community to a family because, although both are groupings and both have boundaries, they are of entirely different orders: I assume that the forces that maintain these two sets of boundaries are completely different from each other, even though they are interrelated and interdependent; furthermore, they serve entirely different, though interrelated and interdependent, goals of the social system. I further assume that units with boundaries that are at the same order of abstraction are comparable. If a community as a boundary-maintaining system among the Midlanders is not comparable at some level with a community as a boundary-maintaining system among the Trobrianders, then we must also come to the conclusion that we cannot compare the family organization of the Midlanders with the family of the Trobrianders.

Boundary-systems within society are not of the same order of abstraction as discrete items of behavior; they are of an entirely different universe than the custom of distending ear lobes with plugs or embroidering arrow quivers. This is an important issue which extends beyond pure theoretical speculation. Without this concept I would not have been able to understand the practice of extrusion *and* its absence, for example, as a way in which parents in a society manipulate the children in relation to the boundaries of the family to inculcate values and a sense of identity.

My second reason comes from the nature of anthropology as a discipline. Anthropology is often called the science of man, not the science of primitive or preliterate man or peasant man alone. It is the study of modern society as well as of preliterate or folk society. To omit modern communities (as representatives of the total culture or society) from a cross-cultural study based primarily on a sample of preliterate and peasant peoples is a kind of discriminatory parochialism that we can scarcely afford on scientific grounds. If the findings of social scientists are truly about people, then they must apply to people everywhere. To make them relevant in this fashion, we need the kinds of theories that enable us to make both broad and specific comparisons between the "simplest" of societies and our own. The theory of boundary-systems is one such attempt in this direction.

There is another side to this picture. Any attempt to construct comparative samples from preliterate and peasant societies only sounds today like a variation on a theme whistled in an empty room. With societies and cultures all over the world taking gigantic leaps in cultural evolution, what is the criterion for deciding when a society is no longer preliterate or peasant? By what standards do you declare that a people have reached the stage of modern technological civilization and are thus no longer comparable with other preliterate and peasant groups?

This, of course, is not to say that everything is comparable. It would be in gross error to imagine that we can compare processes of life in New York City or London with the customary ways of doing things on a Pacific atoll, or in a central highland community in Jamaica. The error does not lie in the fact that we can never really know what goes on in all of New York and London, or that the sizes of these two cities are so much larger than atoll communities or that the ways in which people earn their livelihoods in these separate worlds are so completely different. The error resides in the fact that the boundaries of London and New York City are so distant from the individual and have such little immediate meaning for his daily life and activities that they are of entirely different levels of abstraction than the community boundaries on a Pacific isle or in a Jamaican mountain group. But social scientists do compare the families of London and New York with those of a Pacific island people and a Jamaican mountain community, and they have been doing so very comfortably for many years. They have been able to do this because the boundary-systems are sufficiently similar.

"Science is not any particular method of techniques. It is a way of reasoning. The standards are intellectual rather than procedural. The method of observation, formalization, and testing must vary with the nature of the problem."[14]

CODA

MANY people have sat patiently with me over dining tables, drinks, and desks helping me with problems in connection with this research; they gave freely of their time, energies, and insights. But there are a few whom I want to thank especially for their help.

Dr. Margaret Mead has been encouraging in several ways. She went through an earlier draft of the book twice and gave of herself unstintingly. The germ of the two chapters on incest taboos was originally contained in five manuscript pages in an early chapter. In the summer of 1961, she invited me to develop these ideas into a paper for a "Symposium on Cross-Species Incest Behavior," organized for the Annual Meeting of the American Association for the Advancement of Science, Section H, held in Denver, Colorado, on December 30, 1961. That paper led to the formulations in Chapters 7 and 8.

I have profited from many discussions of this book with Dr. Jan Frank, who answered a number of questions about personality development; his generous criticisms were invaluable. More important, he made the physical writing of the book possible under conditions that would otherwise have made it impossible.

Dr. Lee Rainwater was more than generous with his help. He always managed to find time, no matter how great the pressures of work, to help with a difficult problem and to suggest novel approaches to the analyses of data. Dr. Melford E. Spiro was also kind enough to read the book in manuscript for me.

I wish to acknowledge the courtesy of Prof. Meyer Fortes and of the International African Institute in granting me permission to reproduce Figure 2b from Prof. Fortes' book, *The Web of Kinship Among the Tallensi*, that appears here on page 56.

And last, I want to express my appreciation to my family for being so patient with me whenever my work interrupted our normal course of activities.

NOTES

CHAPTER 1

1. Cohen 1961, 457-516.
2. Dobzhansky 1962, 18, 22.
3. Cohen 1964.

CHAPTER 2

1. WFMH (World Federation of Mental Health) 1957, 16.
2. Cohen 1961, 187-96, 333-5; Hallowell 1955, 75-110.
3. Kluckhohn and Leighton 1946, 54.
4. Leighton and Kluckhohn 1947, 48-9.
5. Op. cit., 51.
6. Kluckhohn 1951, 395, italics omitted.
7. WFMH 1957, 16.
8. Cumming and Cumming 1962, 13.
9. Ibid., 46-7.
10. Cohen 1961, 459-68.
11. Ibid., 329.
12. Aginsky 1940, 43.
13. Hsu 1963, 198-202.
14. Scott 1962, 954.
15. Richards 1948, 86.

CHAPTER 3

1. For some of the possible mechanisms involved in parents' awareness of these non-observable events, see Coult 1963b.
2. Kunstadter 1938, 1950.
3. Kenyon, Knowles and Sandeford 1944.

4. Whitelaw and Foster 1962.
5. Scott 1962. See also, for example, Palmer 1961. Scott contains the most comprehensive bibliography to date on this subject. For work preceding Scott's, see his bibliography.
6. Scott 1962, 951, 952, 955, 957, italics added.

CHAPTER 4

1. Fortes 1949, 53 (Fig. 2b).
1a. Cumming and Cumming 1962, 56.
2. Kluckhohn 1944, 53.
3. For a more extensive discussion of emotional inbreeding, see Cohen 1961, 19-23, 67-70, 330.
4. Gluckman 1955, 55.
5. Loc. cit.
6. Op. cit., 57.
7. Op. cit., 59.
8. The cross-cultural methodology used to test the hypotheses of this study is discussed in Chapter 9.
9. Radcliffe-Brown 1933, 76, 94-5.
10. Ibid., 77.
11. Ibid., 78.
12. Opler 1941, 54, 57.
13. Ibid., 60.
14. Mead 1939b, 44-5; 1940, 198.
15. Spencer and Gillen 1927, 177.
16. Spencer and Gillen 1899, 88.
17. Wagner 1949, 46, 73, 341, 372.
18. Ibid., 40-1.
19. Ashton 1952, 18.
20. Ibid., 18-9, 45, 47.
21. Sheddick 1953, 32.
22. Ashton 1952, 36.
23. Culwick 1935, 338.
24. Ibid., 340.
25. Schapera 1930, 118.
26. Fourie 1928, 89.
27. Ibid., 88-9.
28. Guttman 1932, 3; Raum 1940, 158-9, 168.
29. Raum 1940, 160.

30. Herskovits 1938, 102, 137.
31. *Ibid.*, 277.
32. Flannery 1953, 113-7.
33. *Ibid.*, 111.
34. *Loc. cit.*
35. Titiev 1944, 21.
36. F. Eggan 1950, 48-9.
37. Dennis 1940, 38.
38. Meek 1931, 109.
39. *Ibid.*, 98.
40. *Ibid.*, 82, 97-9.
41. Blackwood 1935, 61.
42. *Ibid.*, 32.
43. *Ibid.*, 44.
44. *Ibid.*, 197.
45. *Ibid.*, 222.
46. *Ibid.*, 199.
47. *Ibid.*, 84.
48. Whiting 1941, 15-9.
49. Doke 1931, 201.
50. *Ibid.*, 140.
51. *Ibid.*, 143.
52. Powdermaker 1933, 56, 91.
53. *Ibid.*, 32.
54. Deacon 1934, 243.
55. *Ibid.*, 16, 41.
56. *Ibid.*, 270.
57. Mead 1930, 32.
58. Mead 1939a, 41.
59. Mead 1930, 42.
60. *Ibid.*, 71; Mead 1939a, 92.
61. Mead 1930, 139.
62. *Loc. cit.*
63. Warner 1937, 70.
64. *Ibid.*, 97.
65. *Ibid.*, 131.
66. *Ibid.*, 53, 127, 137.
67. Kluckhohn and Leighton 1946, 58.
68. Leighton and Kluckhohn 1947, 51.

69. Kluckhohn and Leighton 1946, 48.
70. Joseph, Spicer and Chesky 1949, 126-7.
71. *Ibid.*, 128.
72. *Ibid.*, 153.
73. *Ibid.*, 124.
74. Beaglehole 1938, 278.
75. *Loc. cit.*
76. Fortes 1949, 191-2.
77. *Ibid.*, 140-1
78. *Ibid.*, 142.
79. *Ibid.*, 193-4.
80. *Ibid.*, 63.
81. Linton 1933, 132; 1939, 263.
82. Linton 1933, 297.
83. Junod 1927, 222.
84. *Ibid.*, 232.
85. *Ibid.*, 97, 284.
86. Firth 1936, 148.
87. *Ibid.*, 127.
88. *Ibid.*, 149.
89. *Ibid.*, 158.
90. *Ibid.*, 202.
91. *Ibid.*, 203.
92. *Ibid.*, 204.
93. Malinowski 1922, 71.
94. *Loc. cit.*
95. Malinowski 1935, 36.
96. *Loc. cit.*
97. Du Bois 1944, 75.
98. Belo 1935, 127; 1936, 21.
99. Oberg 1953, 46-8, 65-6.
100. *Ibid.*, 14-5.
101. Mintz 1956, 375.
102. *Ibid.*, 384-5.
103. *Ibid.*, 386.
104. Thompson 1941, 42.
105. *Ibid.*, 46.
106. *Ibid.*, 205.
107. Furer-Haimendorf 1943, 104-5, 108, 127, 157.

108. Wagley 1949, 14-5, 32-3.
109. *Ibid.*, 13.
110. *Ibid.*, 37.
111. Rutter 1929, 62-4.
112. Jenness 1922, 169-70.
113. *Ibid.*, 65-6, 85.
114. Quain 1948, 311-12.
115. Burrows and Spiro 1953, 143-4, 265-72.
116. *Ibid.*, 144.
117. Henry 1941, 49.
118. *Ibid.*, 15, 19, 31, 36-7, 43.
119. Honigmann 1949, 184.
120. *Ibid.*, 124.
121. *Ibid.*, 126.
122. Ford 1941, *passim.*
123. *Ibid.*, 199.
124. Parry 1932, 243.
125. *Ibid.*, 247-8, 394.
126. Gorer 1938, 313-4.
127. *Ibid.*, 63, 306-7; Morris 1938, 211.
128. Linton 1939, 164.
129. *Ibid.*, 150.
130. *Ibid.*, 154.
131. Lynd 1929, 131-52; West 1945, 60, 75-81.
132. Lynd 1929, 110; West 1945, 35, 62.
133. Herskovits 1937, 102-4.
134. Gillin 1947, 98, 101.
135. *Ibid.*, 99.
136. Schapera 1930, 271-2.
137. *Ibid.*, 230.
138. Landes 1937a, 102.
139. Landes 1937b, 13.
140. *Ibid.*, 69.
141. From my personal field notes.
142. Fletcher and La Flesche 1911, 325.
143. *Ibid.*, 330, 337; Dorsey 1884, 226, 273-4.
144. Cohen 1956, 670-2.
145. *Ibid.*, 674.
146. Ray 1932, 131.

147. *Ibid.*, 110.
148. Zborowski and Herzog 1952, 330-4.
149. *Ibid.*, 334-54.
150. Holmberg 1950, 77.
151. *Ibid.*, 57.
152. Honigmann 1946, 84.
153. Embree 1946, 137-44.
154. Yang 1945, 58, 66.
155. *Ibid.*, 63, 128-9.
156. Beals 1946, 102, 175-6.
157. *Ibid.*, 101, 176.
158. MacGregor 1946, 57-8, 110.
159. *Ibid.*, 59, 131.
160. Whiffen 1915, 156.
161. *Ibid.*, 50.
162. Jochelson 1933, 137.
163. A. L. Kroeber, personal communication.
164. Tomasic 1948, 170.

CHAPTER 5

1. Van Gennep 1960, 65-115.
2. Cohen 1961, 351-86.
2a. Young 1962, 381-2.
2b. Brown 1963, 841.
3. Whiting 1962.
4. Scott 1962, 950-5.
5. Cohen 1961, 351-86.
6. Radcliffe-Brown 1933, 94-5.
7. Opler 1941, 134.
8. *Ibid.*, 82.
9. Mead 1939b, 73.
10. *Ibid.*, 96.
11. Spencer and Gillen 1927, 179.
12. Wagner 1949, 351.
13. *Ibid.*, 352.
14. Ashton 1952, 56.
15. Culwick 1935, 342.
16. *Loc. cit.*
17. *Ibid.*, 344.

18. Fourie 1928, 89; Schapera 1930, 118, 125.
19. Raum 1940, 347-8.
20. Herskovits 1938, 299.
21. F. Eggan 1950, 49; Titiev 1944, 116.
22. Blackwood 1935, 222.
23. Whiting 1941, 106.
24. Doke 1931, 148.
25. *Ibid.*, 149.
26. Powdermaker 1933, 102, 138-9.
27. *Ibid.*, 139.
28. Deacon 1934, 260.
29. *Ibid.*, 480, 494.
30. Mead 1930, 35, 91-2; 1939a, 69-70.
31. Warner 1937, 6.
32. Kluckhohn and Leighton 1946, 145.
33. Joseph, Spicer and Chesky 1949, 115-6, 153; Underhill 1939, 163.
34. Beaglehole 1938, 279.
35. *Ibid.*, 280.
36. Fortes 1949, 46, 198, 201.
37. Linton 1933, 296.
38. Junod 1927, 74, 96, 270, 342.
39. *Ibid.*, 177-8.
40. Firth 1936, 423.
41. Du Bois 1944, 80.
42. Covarrubias 1947, 133-6.
43. Margaret Mead, personal communication.
44. Oberg 1953, 65-6.
45. Mintz 1956, 385.
46. Thompson 1941, 41, 210, 224.
47. Furer-Haimendorf 1943, 127.
48. Wagley 1949, 35.
49. Rutter 1929, 73.
50. Jenness 1922, 65-6, 85.
51. Quain 1948, 315.
52. Burrows and Spiro 1953, 288-9.
53. Henry 1941, 36-7, 43.
54. Hongimann 1949, 189.
55. Boas 1897, 341-2; Ford 1941, 34-5.

56. Parry 1932, 394.
57. Gorer 1938, 315.
58. Handy 1923, 93-4.
59. Hollingshead 1949, passim.
60. Herskovits 1937, 101-2.
61. Gillin 1947, 99.
62. Schapera 1930, 272, 279-80.
63. Vedder 1928, 136.
64. Landes 1937b, 15.
65. Landes 1938, 3-5.
66. From my personal field notes.
67. Dorsey 1884, 266; Fletcher and La Flesche 1911, 133.
68. Cohen 1955, passim; 1956, 674.
69. Ray 1932, 133-4.
70. Zborowski and Herzog 1952, 347-8.
71. Ibid., 350.
72. Holmberg 1950, 80.
73. Honigmann 1946, 84-5, 142.
74. Embree 1946, 144-6.
75. Yang 1945, 73.
76. Beals 1946, 176; Foster 1948, 245-7.
77. MacGregor 1946, 139.
78. Whiffen 1915, 157.
79. Priklonskii 1890, Chapter 4, 12-3.
80. Kroeber 1925, 7, 45.
81. Tomasic 1948, 172.

CHAPTER 6

1. Erikson 1962, 7.
2. WFMH 1957, 16.
3. Cohen 1961, 312-50.
4. Radcliffe-Brown 1952.
5. Hoebel 1954, 317-8. For another example of the application of Radcliffe-Brown's view, see Befu and Plotnicov 1962. See also Bohannan 1963, 238-301.
6. Hoebel 1954, 318.
6a. Cohen 1961, 328.
7. Pospisil 1958, 147.

8. See, in this connection, Inkeles 1955 and 1960; Cohen 1961, 96-146.
9. Radcliffe-Brown 1933, 48-50.
10. Opler 1941, 54, 459-60.
11. Margaret Mead, personal communication.
12. Spencer and Gillen 1927, 453.
13. Wagner 1939, 22.
14. Wagner 1940, 217.
15. Sheddick 1953, 42.
16. *Loc. cit.*
17. Culwick 1935, 210-1.
18. Schapera 1930, 154.
19. Guttman 1926, *passim.*
20. Diamond 1951, 29.
21. Flannery 1953, 45.
22. Fred Eggan, personal communication.
23. Meek 1931, 110.
24. Blackwood 1935, 458.
25. Whiting 1941, 124-5.
26. Doke 1931, 63.
27. Powdermaker 1933, 41-2, 304.
28. Deacon 1934, 218.
29. Mead 1930, 43.
30. Warner 1937, 161-2.
31. Kluckhohn and Leighton 1946, 65.
32. Kluckhohn 1944, 65.
33. Underhill 1939, 23.
34. Beaglehole 1938, 246.
35. Fortes 1945, 245.
36. Linton 1933, 153.
37. Junod 1927, 302, 411.
38. Firth 1936, 539-44.
39. Malinowski 1926, 119.
40. Du Bois 1944, 126-7.
41. Bateson and Mead 1942, 259.
42. Covarrubias 1947, 60-1, 64.
43. Oberg 1953, 51.
44. Mintz 1956, 364-7.
45. Thompson 1941, 82-95.

46. Furer-Haimendorf 1943, 95.
47. Wagley 1949, 100-1.
48. Rutter 1929, 135-80.
49. Jennes 1922, 94.
50. Quain 1948, 60-2, 374-428.
51. Burrows and Spiro 1953, 194-8.
52. Henry 1941, 110-1.
53. Honigmann 1949, 149-53.
54. Goldman 1937, 195-8.
55. Parry 1932, 264-5, 269.
56. Gorer 1938, 135-6.
57. Ibid., 139.
58. Handy 1923, 56.
59. Herskovits 1937, 126.
60. Gillen 1947, 92-3.
61. Schapera 1930, 345-6.
62. Landes 1937, 16; 1938, 214-24.
63. From my personal field notes.
64. Dorsey 1884, 369.
65. Cohen 1953, 262-75.
66. Ray 1932, 113.
67. Zborowski and Herzog 1952, 216-8.
68. Holmberg 1950, 60.
69. Honigmann 1946, 66.
70. Embree 1946, 127-8.
71. Yang 1945, 149-50. 166, 242.
72. Beals 1946, 101; Foster 1948, 264.
73. MacGregor 1946, 79, 84.
74. Whiffen 1915, 61, 261.
75. Jochelson 1933, 134; Priklonskii 1890, Chapter 4, 6.
76. Kroeber 1926, passim.
77. Tomasic 1948, 157-62, 184.

CHAPTER 7

1. Beals and Hoijer 1959, 477.
2. For a discussion of some exceptions to the universality of incest taboos, see Middleton 1962.
3. Kaufman 1960, 681.
4. Dowdeswell 1961, 50.

5. For a description of the modern methods used in these observations, together with some of the salient findings, see Christian 1961.
6. Allee 1958, 16.
7. Christian 1961, *passim.*
8. Calhoun 1962, 139.
9. *Ibid.,* 143-4.
10. Allee 1958, 30.
11. Spitz 1945.
12. Bexton, Heron and Scott 1954; Heron 1957; Lilly 1956; Solomon *et al.* 1961.
13. Harlow 1960.
14. Cohen 1961, 486-516.
15. Bergman and Escalona 1949, 333.
16. Freud 1946, 182.
17. Caudill 1962.
18. Catharine McClellan, personal communication.
19. Henry 1936.
20. Hartmann 1953.
21. Frank 1963.
22. Fenichel 1945, 117.
23. Freud 1954, 28-9.
24. *Ibid.,* 29.
25. Fenichel 1945, 204.
26. Erikson 1950, 229.
27. Goode 1963, p. 107.
28. *Op. cit.,* p. 231.
29. *Op. cit.,* p. 285.

CHAPTER 8

1. Cohen 1961, 312-50.
2. *Ibid.,* 351-86.
3. *Ibid.,* 328.
4. Piaget 1948, 86.
5. See the discussion of this by Coult 1963a.
6. For discussions of two different aspects of this problem, see Cohen 1958, and Weinberg 1955, 157-71.
7. Schneider and Gough 1961, 12-3.
8. See Mitchell 1963, who approaches this problem from the

point of view of the hypothesis that the bilateral kindred is a characteristic of all societies.

9. Murdock 1949, 307.
10. *Ibid.*, 308.
11. *Ibid.*, 304-5.
12. *Ibid.*, 302-13.
13. Homans and Schneider 1955.
14. For suggestions that this might be the case, see as examples, Ford and Beach 1952, 176; Beals and Hoijer 1959, 646.
15. Davenport 1959, 562-5.

CHAPTER 9

1. Lewis 1956; Mead 1961, 516-25.
2. Murdock *et al.* 1950.
3. Murdock 1940, 1954, 1957.
4. Cohen 1961, 312-50.
5. *Ibid.*, 351-86.
6. Whiting *et al.* 1958; Burton and Whiting 1961; Whiting 1962; Stephens 1961; Young 1962.
7. Cohen 1964.
8. Whiting and Child 1953, 39-62.
9. Cohen 1953, 413-39.
10. Simpson 1963, 82.
11. Murdock 1957.
12. Murdock *et al.* 1950, xxiii.
13. Whiting 1954, 531.
14. Miller 1949, 291.

BIBLIOGRAPHY

ABERLE, DAVID F., URI BRONFENBRENNER, ECKHARD H. HESS, DANIEL R. MILLER, DAVID M. SCHNEIDER and JAMES N. SPUHLER. 1963. "The Incest Taboo and the Mating Patterns of Animals." *American Anthropologist*, 65: 253-65.

AGINSKY, B. W.
1940. "An Indian's Soliloquy." *American Journal of Sociology*, 46: 43-4.

ALLEE, W. C.
1958. *The Social Life of Animals*. (Rev. ed.) Boston: Beacon Press.

ARENSBERG, CONRAD M.
1954. "The Community-Study Method." *American Journal of Sociology*, 60: 109-24.

ASHTON, HUGO.
1952. *The Basuto*. London: Oxford University Press.

ASIMOV, ISAAC
1962. *The Genetic Code*. New York: New American Library.

BATESON, GREGORY, and MARGARET MEAD.
1942. *Balinese Character: A Photographic Analysis*. New York: New York Academy of Sciences Special Publication.

BEAGLEHOLE, ERNEST
1938. *Ethnology of Pukapuka*. Honolulu: Bernice P. Bishop Museum, Bulletin 105.

BEALS, RALPH
1946. *Cherán: A Sierra Tarascan Village*. Washington, D.C.: Smithsonian Institution, Institute of Social Anthropology, Publication No. 2.

BEALS, RALPH, and HARRY HOIJER
1959. An Introduction to Anthropology. (2nd ed.) New York: Macmillan.

BEFU, HARUMI, and LEONARD PLOTNICOV
1962. "Types of Corporate Unilineal Descent Groups." American Anthropologist, 64: 313-27.

BELO, JANE
1935. "The Balinese Temper." Character and Personality, 4: 120-46.
1936. "A Study of a Balinese Family." American Anthropologist, 38: 12-31.

BENEDICT, RUTH
1938. "Continuities and Discontinuities in Cultural Conditioning." Psychiatry, 1: 161-7.

BERGMAN, PAUL, and SYBILLE K. ESCALONA
1949. "Unusual Sensitivities in Very Young Children." The Psychoanalytic Study of the Child, 3-4: 333-52.

BEXTON, W. H., W. HERON and T. H. SCOTT
1954. "Effects of Decreased Variation in the Sensory Environment." The Canadian Journal of Psychology, 8: 70-6.

BIRDWHISTEL, RAYMOND N.
1958. "Family Structure and Mobility." Transactions of the New York Academy of Sciences, Series II, 21: 136-45.

BLACKWOOD, BEATRICE
1935. Both Sides of Buka Passage: An Ethnographic Study of Social, Sexual, and Economic Questions in the North-Western Solomon Islands. London: Oxford University Press.

BOAS, FRANZ
1897. "The Social Organization and Secret Societies of the Kwakiutl Indians." Washington, D.C.: Report of the U.S. National Museum, 1895, Pt. II, 311-78.

BOSSARD, JAMES H. S., and ELEANOR S. BOLL
1948. "Rite of Passage – A Contemporary Study." Social Forces, 26: 247-55.

Bibliography

BROWN, JUDITH K.
1963. "A Cross-Cultural Study of Female Initiation Rites." American Anthropologist, 65:837-53.

BURROWS, EDWIN G., and MELFORD E. SPIRO
1953. An Atoll Culture: Ethnography of Ifaluk in the Central Carolines. New Haven: Human Relations Area Files Press.

BURTON, RICHARD, and JOHN W. M. WHITING
1961. "The Absent Father and Cross-Sex Identity." Merill-Palmer Quarterly of Behavior and Development, 7: 85-95.

CALHOUN, JOHN B.
1962. "Population Density and Social Pathology." Scientific American, 206: 139-48.

CAUDILL, WILLIAM
1962. "Patterns of Emotion in Modern Japan." In Japanese Culture: Its Development and Characteristics, edited by Robert J. Smith and Richard K. Beardsley, 115-31. Chicago: Aldine Publishing Company.

CHRISTIAN, JOHN J.
1961. "Phenomena Associated with Population Density." Proceedings of the National Academy of Science, 47: 428-49.

COHEN, YEHUDI A.
1953. A Study of Interpersonal Relationships in a Jamaican Community. Unpublished Doctoral Dissertation, Yale University.
1955. "Character Formation and Social Structure in a Jamaican Community." Psychiatry, 18: 275-96.
1956. "Structure and Function: Family Organization and Socialization in a Jamaican Community." American Anthropologist, 58: 664-86.
1958. "Some Aspects of Ritualized Behavior in Interpersonal Relationships." Human Relations, 11: 195-215.
1961. Social Structure and Personality: A Casebook. New York: Holt, Rinehart and Winston.
1962. "Review" of Readings in Cross-Cultural Methodology, edited by Frank W. Moore. American Anthropologist, 64: 853-4.
1964. "The Establishment of Identity in a Social Nexus: The Special Case of Initiation Ceremonies and Their Relationship to Value and Legal Systems." American Anthropologist, 66.

ms. "Macro-ethnology: Large-Scale Comparatives Studies." In Introduction to Cultural Antropology: Essays in the Scope and Method of the Science of Man, edited by James A. Clifton. Forthcoming. Boston: Houghton Mifflin.

COULT, ALLAN D.
1963a. "Causality and Cross-Sex Prohibitions." American Anthropologist, 65: 266-77.
1963b. "Unconscious Inference and Cultural Origins." American Anthropologist, 65: 32-5.

COVARRUBIAS, MIGUEL
1947. Island of Bali. New York: Alfred A. Knopf.

CRICK, F. H. C.
1962. "The Genetic Code." Scientific American, 207: No. 4, 66-74.
1963. "On the Genetic Code." Science, 139: 461-4.

CULWICK, A. T. and G. J.
1935. Ubena of the Rivers. London: Allen and Unwin.

CUMMING, JOHN and ELAINE
1962. Ego and Milieu: Theory and Practice of Environmental Therapy. New York: Atherton Press.

DAVENPORT, WILLIAM
1959. "Nonunilinear Descent and Descent Groups." American Anthropologist, 61: 557-72.

DEACON, A. BERNARD
1934. Malekula: A Vanishing People in the New Hebrides. London: Routledge & Kegan Paul.

DENNIS, WAYNE
1940. The Hopi Child. New York: Appleton-Century.

DEUTSCH, HELENE
1945. The Psychology of Women: A Psychoanalytic Interpretation. 2 vols. New York: Grune and Stratton.

DIAMOND, STANLEY
1951. Dahomey: A Proto-State in West Africa. Unpublished Doctoral Dissertation, Columbia University.

Bibliography

DOBZAHNSKY, THEODOSIUS
1962. *Mankind Evolving: Evolution of the Human Species.* New Haven: Yale University Press.

DOKE, CLEMENT M.
1931. *The Lambas of Northern Rhodesia: A Study of Their Customs and Beliefs.* London: George Harrap.

DORSEY, J. O.
1884. "Omaha Sociology." Washington, D.C.: *Third Annual Report of the Bureau of American Ethnology,* 205-370.

DOWDESWELL, W. H.
1961. *Animal Ecology.* New York: Harper Torch Books.

DuBois, CORA
1944. *The People of Alor: A Socio-Psychological Study of an East Indian Island.* Minneapolis: University of Minnesota Press.

DURKHEIM, EMIL
1947a. *The Elementary Forms of Religious Life.* Glencoe, Ill. The Free Press.
1947b. *The Division of Labor in Society.* Glencoe, Ill. The Free Press.

EGGAN, DOROTHY
1956. "Instruction and Affect in Hopi Cultural Continuity." *Southwestern Journal of Anthropology,* 12: 347-70.

EGGAN, FRED
1950. *Social Organization of the Western Pueblos.* Chicago: University of Chicago Press.

EISENSTADT, S. N.
1956. *From Generation to Generation: Age Groups and Social Structure.* Glencoe, Ill.: The Free Press.

EMBREE, JOHN
1946. *A Japanese Village: Suye Mura.* London: Routledge & Kegan Paul.

ERIKSON, ERIK H.
1950. *Childhood and Society.* New York: Norton.

[231]

1962. "Youth: Fidelity and Diversity." *Daedalus: Journal of the American Academy of Arts and Sciences*, Winter: 5-27.

EVANS-PRITCHARD, E. E.
1940. *The Nuer: A Description of the Modes of Livelihood and Political Institutions of a Nilotic People*. Oxford: Oxford University Press.

FENICHEL, OTTO
1945. *The Psychoanalytic Theory of Neurosis*. New York: Norton.

FIRTH, RAYMOND
1936. *We, The Tikopia: A Sociological Study of Kinship in Primitive Polynesia*. London: Allen and Unwin.
1951a. "Contemporary British Social Anthopology." *American Anthropologist*, 53: 474-89.
1951b. *Elements of Social Organization*. New York: Philosophical Library.

FLANNERY, REGINA
1953. *The Gros Ventres of Montana. Part I. Social Life*. Washington, D.C.: The Catholic University of America Anthropological Series, No. 15.

FLETCHER, ALICE C., and FRANCIS LaFLESCHE
1911. "The Omaha Tribe." Washington, D.C.: *27th Annual Report of the Bureau of American Ethnology*, 17-654.

FORD, CLELLAN S.
1941. *Smoke from Their Fires: The Life of a Kwakiutl Chief*. New Haven: Yale University Press.

FORD, C. S., and F. A. BEACH
1952. *Patterns of Sexual Behavior*. New York: Harper.

FORTES, MEYER
1945. *The Dynamics of Clanship among the Tallensi*. London: Oxford University Press.
1949. *The Web of Kinship among the Tallensi*. London: Oxford University Press.
1953. "The Structure of Unilineal Descent Groups." *American Anthropologist*, 55: 17-41.

Bibliography

FOSTER, GEORGE
1948. *Empire's Children: The People of Tzintzuntzan.* Washington, D.C.: Smithsonian Institution, Institute of Social Anthropology, Publication No. 6.

FOURIE, L.
1928. "The Bushman in Southwest Africa," *In The Native Tribes of South West Africa,* 79-104. Cape Town: Cape Times, Ltd.

FRANK, JAN
1962. "Communication and Empathy." In *Proceedings of the Third World Congress of Psychiatry.* Toronto: University of Toronto Press and McGill University Press.

FREUD, ANNA
1946. *The Ego and the Mechanisms of Defense.* New York: International Universities Press.
1954. "Discussion" of "Problems of Infantile Neurosis," by Phyllis Greenacre. *The Psychoanalytic Study of the Child,* 9: 16-71.
1958. "Adolescence." *The Psychoanalytic Study of the Child,* 13: 255-78.

FURER-HAIMENDORF, CHRISTOPH VON
1943. *The Chenchus: Jungle Folk of the Deccan.* London: Macmillan.

GILLIN, JOHN
1947. *Moche: A Peruvian Coastal Community.* Washington, D.C.: Smithsonian Instition, Institute of Social Anthropology, Publication No. 3.

GLUCKMAN, MAX
1955. *Custom and Conflict in Africa.* Glencoe, Ill.: The Free Press

GOLDMAN, IRVING
1937. "The Kwakiutl of Vancouver Island," In *Cooperation and Competition Among Primitive Peoples,* edited by Margaret Mead, 180-209. New York: McGraw-Hill.

GOODE, WILLIAM J.
1963. *World Revolution and Family Patterns.* New York: The Free Press of Glencoe.

GORER, GEOFFREY
1938. *Himalayan Village: An Account of the Lepchas of Sikkim.* London: Michael Joseph.

GREENACRE, PHYLLIS
1950. "The Prepuberty Trauma in Girls." *The Psychoanalytic Quarterly,* 19; reprinted in *Trauma, Growth, and Personality.* New York: Norton (1952).

GUTTMAN, BRUNO
1926. *Das Recht der Dschagga.* Munich: Beck.
1932. *Die Stammeslehren der Chagga.* Munich: Beck.

HANDY, E. S. CRAIGHILL
1923. *The Native Culture in the Marquesas.* Honolulu; Bernice P. Bishop Museum, Bulletin 9.

HARLOW, H. F.
1958. "The Nature of Love." *American Psychologist,* 13: 673-85.

HARTLAND, E. S.
1924. *Primitive Law.* London: Methuen.

HARTMANN, HEINZ
1953. "Contribution to the Metapsychology of Schizophrenia." *The Psychoanalytic Study of the Child,* 8: 177-88.
1959. *Ego Psychology and the Problem of Adaption.* New York: International Universities Press.

HARTMANN, HEINZ, ERNST KRIS and RUDOLPH LOEWENSTEIN
1946. "Comments on the Formation of the Psychic Structure." *The Psychoanalytic Study of the Child,* 2: 11-38.

HENRY, JULES
1936. "The Personality of the Kaingang Indians." *Character and Personality,* 5: 113-23.
1941. *Jungle People: The Kaingang Tribe of the Highlands of Brazil.* New York: J. J. Augustin.

HERON, W.
1957. "The Pathology of Boredom." *Scientific American,* 196, 52-6. Reprinted in Larabee, Eric, and Rolf Meyersohn, *Mass Leisure,* 136-41. Glencoe, Ill.: The Free Press (1958).

Bibliography

HERSKOVITS, MELVILLE J.
1937. *Life in a Haitian Valley*. New York: Alfred A. Knopf.
1938. *Dahomey: An Ancient West African Kingdom*. New York: J. J. Augustin.

HOEBEL, E. ADAMSON
1954. *The Law of Primitive Man: A Study in Comparative Legal Dynamics*. Cambridge: Harvard University Press.
1958. *Man in the Primitive World: An Introduction to Anthropology*. New York: McGraw-Hill.

HOLLINGSHEAD, AUGUST B.
1949. *Elmtown's Youth: The Impact of Social Classes on Adolescents*. New York: Wiley.

HOLMBERG, ALAN
1950. *Nomads of the Long Bow: The Siriono of Eastern Bolivia*. Washington, D.C.: Smithsonian Instition, Institute of Social Anthropology, Publication No. 10.

HOMANS, GEORGE C., and DAVID M. SCHNEIDER
1955. *Marriage Authority and Final Causes: A Study of Unilateral Cross-Cousin Marriage*. Glencoe, Ill.: The Free Press.

HONIGMANN, JOHN J.
1946. *Ethnography and Acculturation of the Fort Nelson Slave*. New Haven: Yale University Publications in Anthropology, No. 33.
1949. *Culture and Ethos of Kaska Society*. New Haven: Yale University Publications in Anthropology, No. 40.

HSU, FRANCIS L. K.
1963. *Clan, Caste and Club: A Study of Chinese, Hindu, and American Ways of Life*. Princeton: Van Nostrand.

INKELES, ALEX
1955. "Social Change and Social Character: The Role of Parental Mediation." *Journal of Social Issues*, 11 No. 2: 12-23.
1960. "Industrial Man: The Relation of Status to Experience, Perception, and Value." *American Journal of Sociology*, 66: 1-31.

JACKSON, DON
1960. *The Etiology of Schizophrenia*. New York: Basic Books.

JENNESS, DIAMOND
1922. "The Life of the Copper Eskimos." Ottawa: Report of the Canadian Arctic Expedition, 12: Part A.

JOCHELSON, WALDEMAR
1933. "The Yakut." Anthropological Papers of the American Museum of Natural History, 33: Part II, 35-225.

JOSEPH, ALICE, ROSAMOND B. SPICER and JANE CHESKY
1949. The Desert People: A Study of the Papago. Chicago: University of Chicago Press.

JUNOD, HENRI
1927. The Life of a South African Tribe. Vol. 1. London: Macmillan.

KAUFMAN, I. CHARLES
1960. "Some Ethological Studies of Social Relationships and Conflict Situations." Journal of The American Psychoanalytic Association, 8: 671-85.

KAY, BRIAN
1957. "The Reliability of HRAF Coding Procedures." American Anthropologist, 59: 524-7.

KENYON, A. T., K. KNOWLTON and I. SANDEFORD
1944. "The Anabolic Effects of the Androgens and Somatic Growth in Man." Annals of Internal Medicine, 20: 632-54.

KINSEY, ALFRED C. et al.
1953. Sexual Behavior in the Human Female. Philadelphia: Saunders.

KLUCKHOHN, CLYDE
1944. Navaho Witchcraft. Papers of the Peabody Museum of American Archaeology and Ethnology, 22: No. 2. Cambridge: Harvard University.
1951. "Values and Value-Orientations in the Theory of Action: An Exploration in Definition and Classification." In Toward a General Theory of Action, edited by Talcott Parsons and Edward A. Shils, 388-433. Cambridge: Harvard University Press.
1955. "Anthropology." In What is Science?, edited by James R. Newman, 315-57. New York: Simon and Schuster.

Bibliography

KLUCKHOHN, CLYDE, and DOROTHEA LEIGHTON
1946. *The Navaho*. Cambridge: Harvard University Press.

KROEBER, A. L.
1925. *Handbook of the Indians of California*. Washington, D.C.: Bureau of American Ethnology, Bulletin 78.
1926. "Yurok Law." Rome: *Proceedings of the 22nd International Congress of Americanists*, 511-16.

KUNSTADTER, RALPH H.
1938. "The Induction of Primitive Puberty with Androgenic Substances." *Endocrinology*, 23: 661-5.
1950. "The Nutritional and Endocrine Control of Growth in Children." In *Progress in Clinical Endocrinology*, edited by Samuel Loskin, 518-24. New York: Grune and Stratton.

LABARRE, WESTON
1954. *The Human Animal*. Chicago: University of Chicago Press.

LANDES, RUTH
1937a. "The Ojibwa of Canada." In *Cooperation and Competition Among Primitive Peoples*, edited by Margaret Mead, 87-126. New York: McGraw-Hill.
1937a. *Ojibwa Sociology*. New York: Columbia University Contributions to Anthropology, Vol. 29.
1938. *The Ojibwa Woman*, New York: Columbia University Contributions to Anthropology, Vol. 31.

LEIGHTON, DOROTHEA, and CLYDE KLUCKHOHN
1947. *Children of the People: The Navaho Individual and His Development*. Cambridge: Harvard University Press.

LEVI-STRAUSS, CLAUDE
1956. "The Family." In *Man, Culture, and Society*, edited by Harry L. Shapiro, 261-85. New York: Oxford University Press.

LEWIS, OSCAR
1951. *Life in a Mexican Village: Tepoztlan Restudied*. Urbana: University of Illinois Press.
1956. "Comparisons in Cultural Anthropology." In *Current Anthropology: A Supplement to Anthropology Today*, edited by William L. Thomas, Jr., 259-92. Chicago: University of Chicago Press.

1960. *Tepoztlan: Village in Mexico.* New York: Holt, Rinehart and Winston.

LILLY, JOHN C.
1956. "Mental Effects of Reduction of Ordinary Length of Physical Stimuli on Intact, Healthy Persons." *Psychiatric Reports,* 5: 1-9.

LINTON, RALPH
1933. *The Tanala: A Hill Tribe in Madagascar.* Chicago: Anthropological Series, Field Museum of Natural History, Vol. 22.
1936. *The Study of Man: An Introduction.* New York: Appleton-Century.
1939a. "The Tanala of Madagascar." In *The Individual and His Society,* edited by Abram Kardiner, 251-90. New York: Columbia University Press.
1939b. "Marquean Culture." In *The Individual and His Society,* edited by Abram Kardiner, 137-96. New York: Columbia University Press.
1942. "Age and Sex Categories." *American Sociological Review,* 7: 589-603.

LOWIE, ROBERT H.
1947. *Primitive Society.* New York: Liveright.

LYND, ROBERT S. and HELEN M.
1929. *Middletown: A Study in American Culture.* New York: Harcourt, Brace.

MACGREGOR, GORDON
1946. *Warriors Without Weapons.* Chicago: University of Chicago Press.

MAHLER, MARGARET S.
1952. "On Child Psychosis and Schizophrenia: Autistic and Symbiotic Infantile Psychoses." *The Psychoanalytic Study of the Child,* 7: 286-305.

MAINE, SIR HENRY
1931. *Ancient Law.* London: Oxford University Press.

MALINOWSKI, BRONISLAW
1922. *Argonauts of the Western Pacific.* London: Routledge & Kegan Paul

[238]

1926. *Crime and Custom in Savage Society.* London: Routledge & Kegan Paul.
1935. *Coral Gardens and Their Magic.* Vol. 1. London: Allen & Unwin.

MAY, ROLLO
1950. *The Meaning of Anxiety.* New York: Ronald Press.

MEAD, MARGARET
1930. *Social Organization of Manua.* Honolulu: Bernice P. Bishop Museum, Bulletin 76.
1939a. *Coming of Age in Samoa.* Reprinted in *From the South Seas.* New York: Morrow.
1939b. *Sex and Temperament in Three Primitive Societies.* Reprinted in *From the South Seas.* New York: Morrow.
1940. "The Mountain Arapesh. III. Socio-Economic Life." *Anthropological Papers of the American Museum of Natural History,* 40: Part III, 163-232.
1941. "Back of Adolescence Lies Early Childhood." *Childhood Education,* 18: 58-61.

MEAD, MARGARET (ed.)
1961. *Cooperation and Competition among Primitive Peoples.* Rev. paperback ed. Boston: Beacon Press.

MEEK, C. K.
1931. *A Sudanese Kingdom: An Ethnological Study of the Jukun-Speaking People of Nigeria.* London: Routledge & Kegan Paul.

MERCIER, P.
1954. "The Fon of Dahomey." In *African Worlds: Studies in the Cosmological Ideas and Social Values of African Peoples,* edited by Daryll Forde, 210-34. New York: Oxford University Press.

MERTON ROBERT K.
1957. *Social Theory and Social Structure.* Rev. and enlarged ed. Glencoe, Ill.: The Free Press.

MIDDLETON, RUSSELL
1962. "Brother-Sister and Father-Daughter Marriage in Ancient Egypt." *American Sociological Review,* 27: 603-12.

MILLER, EDGAR G., JR.
1949. "Scientific Method and Social Problems." *Science*, 109: 290-1.

MINTZ, SIDNEY
1956. "Cañamelar: The Subculture of a Rural Sugar Proletariat." In *The People of Puerto Rico: A Study in Social Anthropology*, edited by Julian Steward, 314-417. Urbana: University of Illinois Press.

MITCHELL, WILLIAM E.
1963. "Theoretical Problems in the Concept of Kindred." *American Anthropologist*, 65: 343-54.

MORRIS, JOHN
1938. *Living With Lepchas: A Book About the Sikkim Himalayas*. London: Heinemann.

MURDOCK, GEORGE P.
1934. *Our Primitive Contemporaries*. New York: Macmillan.
1940. "The Cross Cultural Survey." *American Sociological Review*, 5: 361-70.
1949. *Social Structure*. New York: Macmillan.
1954. "Sociology and Anthropology." In *For a Science of Social Man*, edited by John Gillin, 14-32. New York: Macmillan.
1957. "World Ethnographic Sample." *American Anthropologist*, 59:664-87.

MURDOCK, GEORGE P. et al.
1950. *Outline of Cultural Materials*. 3rd rev. ed. New Haven: Human Relations Area Files Press.

MURPHY, GARDNER
1947. *Personality: A Biosocial Approach to Origins and Structure*. New York: Harper.

NADEL, S. F.
1951. *The Foundations of Social Anthropology*. Glencoe, Ill.: The Free Press.
1957. *The Theory of Social Structure*. Glencoe, Ill.: The Free Press.

OBERG, KALVERO
1953. *Indian Tribes of Northern Matto Grosso, Brazil*. Washing-

ton, D.C.: Smithsonian Institution, Institute of Social Anthropology, Publication No. 15.

OPLER, MORRIS P.
1941. *An Apache Life-Way: The Economic, Social, and Religious Institutions of the Chiricahua Indians.* Chicago: University of Chicago Press.

PALMER, FRANCIS H.
1961. "Critical Periods of Development: Report on a Conference." *Items, Social Science Research Council,* 15: 13-18.

PARRY, N. E.
1932. *The Lakhers.* London: Macmillan.

PARSONS, TALCOTT
1951. *The Social System.* Glencoe, Ill.: The Free Press.

PIAGET, JEAN
1948. *The Moral Judgment of the Child.* Glencoe, Ill.: The Free Press.

POSPISIL, LEOPOLD
1958. *Kapauku Papuans and Their Law.* New Haven: Yale University Publications in Anthropology, No. 54.

POWDERMAKER, HORTENSE
1933. *Life in Lesu: The Study of a Melanesian Society in New Ireland.* New York: Norton.

PRIKLONSKII, V.
1890. *The Years in Yakut Territory.* Translated and reprinted in *Yakut Ethnographic Sketches* (1953). New Haven: Human Relations Area Files Press.

QUAIN, BUELL
1948. *Fijian Village.* Chicago: University of Chicago Press.

RADCLIFFE-BROWN, A. R.
1933. *The Andaman Islanders.* Cambridge: Cambridge University Press.
1935. "Patrilineal and Matrilineal Succession." *The Iowa Law Review,* Vol. 20. Reprinted in *Structure and Function in Primitive*

[241]

Society: *Essays and Addresses* of A. R. Radcliffe Brown, 32-48. Glencoe, Ill.: The Free Press.
1950. "*Introduction*" to *African Systems of Kinship and Marriage*, edited by A. R. Radcliffe-Brown and D. Forde, 1-85. London: Oxford University Press.
1952. "Primitive Law" (Originally published in 1933). Reprinted in *Structure and Function in Primitive Society: Essays and Addresses* of A. R. Radcliffe-Brown, 212-19. Glencoe, Ill.: The Free Press.

RAUM, OTTO
1940. *Chagga Childhood*. London: Oxford University Press.

RAY, VERNE F.
1932. *The Sanpoil and Nespelem: Salishan Peoples of Northeastern Washington*. Seattle: University of Washington Publications in Anthropology, Vol. 5.

RICHARDS, AUDREY I.
1948. *Hunger and Work in a Savage Society: A Functional Study of Nutrition among the Southern Bantu.* Glencoe, Ill.: The Free Press.

RUTTER, OWEN
1929. *The Pagans of North Borneo*. London: Hutchinson.

SCHAPERA, I.
1930. *The Khoisan Peoples of South Africa*. London: Routledge & Kegan Paul.
1938. *A Handbook of Tswana Law and Custom*. London: Oxford University Press.

SCHNEIDER, DAVID M., and KATHLEEN GOUGH
1961. *Matrilineal Kinship*. Berkeley and Los Angeles: University of California Press.

SCOTT, J. P.
1962. "Critical Periods in Behavioral Development." *Science*, 138: 949-58.

SHEDDICK, F. G. J.
1953. *The Southern Sotho*. London: International African Institute.

Bibliography

SIMPSON, GEORGE G.
1963: "Biology and the Nature of Science." Science, 139: 81-8.

SOLOMON, PHILIP, et al.
1961. Sensory Deprivation. Cambridge: Harvard University Press.

SPENCER, BALDWIN, and F. J. GILLEN
1899. Native Tribes of Central Australia. London: Macmillan.
1927. The Arunta. London: Macmillan.

SPITZ, RENE A.
1945. "Hospitalism: An Inquiry Into the Genesis of Psychiatric Conditions in Early Childhood." The Psychoanalytic Study of the Child, 1: 53-74.

STEPHENS, WILLIAM
1961. The Oedipus Complex. New York: The Free Press.

THOMPSON, LAURA
1941. Guam and Its People: A Study of Culture Change and Colonial Education. Princeton: Princeton University Press.

TITIEV, MISCHA
1944. Old Oraibi: A Study of the Hopi Indians of Third Mesa. Cambridge: Papers of the Peabody Museum of American Archaeology and Ethnology, 22: No. 1.

TOMASIC, DINKO
1948. Personality and Culture in Eastern European Politics. New York: Stewart.

UNDERHILL, RUTH
1939. Social Organization of the Papago Indians. New York: Columbia University Contributions in Anthropology, Vol. 30.

VAN GENNEP, ARNOLD
1959. The Rites of Passage (translated by Monika Vizedom and G. L. Caffee). Chicago: University of Chicago Press.

VEDDER, H.
1928. "The Nama." In The Native Tribes of South West Africa, 107-52. Cape Town: Cape Times, Ltd.

WAGLEY, CHARLES
1949. *The Social and Religious Life of a Guatemalan Village.* Washington, American Anthropological Association. Memoir 71.

WAGNER, GUNTER
1939. "The Changing Family Among the Bantu Kavirondo." *Africa*, 12: Supp.
1940. "The Political Organization of the Bantu of Kavirondo," In *African Political Systems*, edited by M. Fortes and E. E. Evans-Pritchard, 165-96. London: Oxford University Press.
1949. *The Bantu of North Kavirondo.* Vol. 1. London. Oxford University Press.

WARNER, W. LLOYD
1937. *A Black Civilization: A Social Study of an Australian Tribe.* New York: Harper.

WATSON, J. D.
1963. "Involvement of RNA in the Synthesis of Proteins." *Science*, 140: 17-26.

WEINBERG, S. KIRSON
1955. *Incest Behavior.* New York: Citadel.

WEST, JAMES
1945. *Plainville, U. S. A.* New York: Columbia University Press.

WHIFFEN, THOMAS
1915. *The North-West Amazons: Notes of Some Months Spent Among Cannibal Tribes.* London: Constable.

WHITELAW, M. JAMES, and THOMAS N. FOSTER
1962. "Treatment of Excessive Height in Girls." *The Journal of Pediatrics*, 61: 556-70.

WHITING, JOHN W. M.
1941. *Becoming a Kwoma: Teaching and Learning in a New Guinea Tribe.* New Haven: Yale University Press.
1954. "The Cross-Cultural Method." In *Handbook of Social Psychology*, edited by Gardner Lindsey, I: 523-31. Cambridge: Addison-Wesley.
1962. "Comment" (on Young 1962). *American Journal of Sociology*, 67: 391-4.

WHITING, JOHN W. M., and IRVIN L. CHILD
1953. *Child Training and Personality: A Cross Cultural Study.* New Haven: Yale University Press.

WHITING, JOHN W. M., RICHARD KLUCKHOHN and ALBERT ANTHONY.
1958. "The Function of Male Initiation Ceremonies at Puberty." In *Readings in Social Psychology,* 3rd ed., edited by Eleanor E. Maccoby, Theodore M. Newcomb, and Eugene Hartley, 359-70. New York: Holt, Rinehart and Winston.

WILSON, MONICA
1951. *Good Company: A Study of Nyakyusa Age Villages.* London: Oxford University Press.

WORLD FEDERATION OF MENTAL HEALTH
1957. *Identity.* London World Federation of Mental Health, Introductory Study No. 1.

YANG, MARTIN C.
1945. *A Chinese Village: Taitou, Shantung Province.* New York. Columbia University Press.

YOUNG, FRANK W.
1962. "The Function of Male Initiation Ceremonies: A Cross Cultural Test of an Alternative Hypothesis." *American Journal of Sociology,* 67: 379-91.

ZBOROWSKI, MARK, and ELIZABETH HERZOG
1952. *Life Is With People: The Jewish Little-Town of Eastern Europe.* New York: International Universities Press.

INDEX

INDEX

For Product Safety Concerns and Information please contact our EU
representative GPSR@taylorandfrancis.com Taylor & Francis Verlag GmbH,
Kaufingerstraße 24, 80331 München, Germany

Batch number: 08153776

Printed by Printforce, the Netherlands